Puffin

Pets fo

If you're planning to get a there are some important questions to ask. How big will it grow? How much will it eat and how often? How should it be housed? After all, what starts off as an adorable little puppy could grow into an enormous dog that's totally unsuitable for your high-rise flat. But then again, you can't take a goldfish for walks...

In this book, Dick King-Smith (presenter of the Sunday morning animal spot on *TV-am*'s 'Rub-a-dub-tub' and one of Puffin's most popular authors) tells you all you need to know about twelve different animals that can make great pets – provided they are sensibly and lovingly cared for. As well as lots of stories about the author's own pets (the cover photograph shows Dick with two of his favourites, Dodo the Dachshund and Frank the French Lop rabbit), the book also contains over fifty illustrations. Whether you want to know the correct way to pick up a gerbil, how to trim your budgie's claws, which wild plants are suitable for rabbits to eat, how to house-train your puppy or even how to get a broody bantam hen to hatch out chicks – or whether you just want to find out more about animals, *Pets for Keeps* makes practical and fascinating reading.

Illustrated by Alan Saunders

Other books by Dick King-Smith

Daggie Dogfoot
The Fox Busters
Harry's Mad
Magnus Powermouse
The Mouse Butcher
The Queen's Nose
The Sheep-Pig

Pets for Keeps

Dick King-Smith

PUFFIN BOOKS

Puffin Books, Penguin Books Ltd, Harmondsworth, Middlesex, England
Viking Penguin Inc., 40 West 23rd Street, New York, New York 10010, U.S.A.
Penguin Books Australia Ltd, Ringwood, Victoria, Australia
Penguin Books Canada Limited, 2801 John Street, Markham, Ontario, Canada L3R 1B4
Penguin Books (N.Z.) Ltd, 182–190 Wairau Road, Auckland 10, New Zealand

First published 1986

Copyright © Dick King-Smith, 1986
Illustrations copyright © Alan Saunders, 1986
All rights reserved

Made and printed in Great Britain by
Cox & Wyman Ltd, Reading

Typeset in Sabon by
Rowland Phototypesetting Ltd
Bury St Edmunds, Suffolk

Except in the United States of America, this book is sold subject
to the condition that it shall not, by way of trade or otherwise, be lent,
re-sold, hired out, or otherwise circulated without the
publisher's prior consent in any form of binding or cover other than
that in which it is published and without a similar condition
including this condition being imposed on the subsequent purchaser

Contents

    Foreword 1
1 Budgerigars 5
2 Hamsters 12
3 Cats 22
4 Guinea-pigs 33
5 Mice 47
6 Rabbits 57
7 Gerbils 71
8 Canaries 80
9 Bantams 90
10 Rats 103
11 Goldfish 113
12 Dogs 123
    Further reading 138

Foreword

I've still got a very old book, a book that was already old when I was a small boy. It's called *Pets and How to Keep Them*, and it's very bashed about and dog-eared, with some of the pages loose and some of the ideas in it rather out of date because it was written in 1907.

But the man who wrote it had thought quite a lot about what the word 'pet' means: an animal that is special to you, a favourite.

Yet it's not enough just to be fond of your pet. You can be fond of your old teddy-bear, but he can't become hungry or thirsty or unhappy. Your pet can, if you don't look after it properly. You don't have to be an expert – I'm not – but there are some things you need to know before you start, and I don't simply mean how to house it or what to feed it.

Buying a pet is a pretty serious business, something you want to think very carefully about before you do it. Why? Because whatever pet you choose, large or small, intelligent or bird-brained, warm-blooded or cold-blooded, furred or feathered, you then become responsible for a living, breathing, feeling animal.

If you get fed up with the toy you were given for Christmas or your birthday, you can give it away or chuck it away or just stick it in the cupboard and forget about it. But an animal relies solely on you to keep it alive, healthy and contented. It cannot tell you in words when it is hungry or cold or ill or just plain miserable. You have to make sure, as far as you can, that it is never any of these things.

Certainly your pet is something to give you pleasure and amusement, but it's not just a plaything. It's an individual. It's an individual, what's more, that has to trust and rely upon you. It doesn't care if you're fat or thin, or good at football or rotten at spelling – it just needs you, your care, your interest, your affection, for the whole of its life. That life may be quite a short one, like a hamster's, but it may be a very long one. It's not uncommon for dogs and cats to live for fifteen or even twenty years. And at the end of that life, long or short, you want to be able to look back and think that you made it as happy as possible.

Of the hundreds of pets that I've kept, three are buried in my garden. Old Jinks, the ginger cat, lies under a flagstone in the little courtyard outside the back door, and beneath my only apple tree are two of my favourite Abyssinian guinea-pigs. On one side lies King Arthur, who was golden, and on the other the blue roan, Beach Boy. All three died peacefully of old age after long and pleasant lives, and that's the best that anybody can hope for.

That old book of mine had hundreds of different animals in it, some quite large, some rather rare. For this book, I've just chosen a few, smallish and ordinary.

Whichever kind you pick for yourself, I hope you'll be happy with it. Make sure it's happy with you.

1 Budgerigars

My cousin had a talking budgie called Charlie Bingham. He wasn't a very good talker. All he could say was, 'My name is Charlie Bingham.'

Charlie was tame and flew freely about the house. All day long, in one room or another, you would hear his tinny little voice, telling you over and over again that his name was Charlie Bingham.

One day a friend came to lunch, bringing with him his Jack Russell Terrier. 'Anyone seen Charlie lately?' asked someone, as the family sat round the table. Then suddenly there came from underneath it a growl and the sound of a scuffle. There was a long moment's silence, and then that tinny little voice said, for the last time, 'My name . . . is Charlie . . . Bingham.'

Budgerigars are probably the easiest of all pet birds to look after

6 Pets for Keeps

Poor Charlie. I'm sure your bird will have a longer life with a happier ending.

Budgerigars are probably the easiest of all pet birds to look after. They're not terribly expensive to buy or to feed; they're colourful and chatty (in their own language and even in yours). But I think it's also easy to treat a budgie thoughtlessly.

With the best of intentions people stick a single bird into the usual kind of wire cage that you hang up,

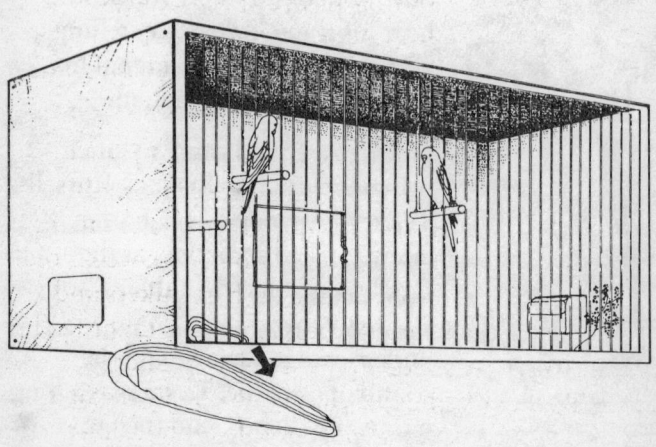

Budgies need a solid, draught-proof cage with plenty of room, a few perches, and containers for food and water. Most budgies enjoy nibbling at a cuttlefish bone

a cage that they then fill with ladders and swings and bells and mirrors and even a model plastic budgie too.

To begin with, I think that birds are happier in a solid cage, with wooden sides and top, and wire in the front only. A cage like that is draught-proof, and birds feel more relaxed in it than when they're hung in the middle of a room (especially if one of your other pets is a cat). Also, the average wire cage is small enough already, without filling it with toys. All the budgie needs is plenty of room, a few perches of different sizes, containers for food and water, and, the best toy of all, another budgie.

The only sensible reason for keeping a single budgerigar is to teach it to talk. This means buying a young bird, around six weeks old (cocks make the best talkers and hens the best biters), so that it will listen to your voice and not to budgie chatter. Probably the first thing most people try to teach a bird is its name, and here's a good tip about that. The *ee* sound is one that budgies copy best, so it's not a

8 Pets for Keeps

bad idea to choose a name that uses it, like *P*eter. Also, if you have a bird on its own, you can get it finger-tame and perhaps allow it to fly freely sometimes. Always remember Charlie Bingham though.

But generally I think it's best to have a big, solid cage with a couple of birds in it, for company. Choose two cock birds if you can — you can tell the sexes apart by the colour of the *cere*, a fleshy patch just above the beak. The cere of a young cock has a bluish tinge, while a young hen's is pinkish. An adult cock's cere is quite blue, an adult hen's brown, even chocolate-coloured. And try to buy from a breeder. The birds will have been handled and so be calmer than those bought in a pet shop, and you can be that much surer of buying young healthy stock. (Breeder's addresses can be found in the magazines listed in the Checklists at the end of each chapter.)

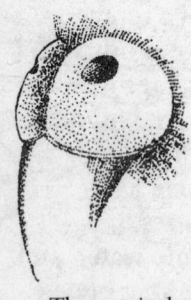

The *cere* is the fleshy patch just above the budgie's beak

Always look for a bird with a bright eye and with plenty of flat, clean, shiny feathering. See that the budgie is active, flying about and feeding. And count its toes (three front and one back on each foot) because sometimes they lose one.

Colour doesn't matter a bit. There are dozens of different shades – blue and yellow and mixtures of colours – but I always think a green bird, the colour of the wild budgies in their native Australia, is as handsome as any.

Feeding's easy. All you need is one container for clean water and another for seed; a mixture of canary seed and millet is best. Check and fill the hoppers every day, remembering that budgerigars cannot go without food for long. You can buy millet in sprays too, which they like, and some greenfood is good for them. Give a little bit of apple or lettuce or dandelion, but don't give too much and don't leave it to get stale. As well as grit, which budgies need to help them digest their food, it's a good idea to have a bit of cuttlefish bone and a mineral block in the cage for them to nibble at – budgies are great nibblers. Incidentally, don't worry if they choose not to use these – some just don't fancy them.

Finally, buy some sand – special bird-sand – to spread on the floor of the cage, and change it regularly; you may find it better to buy ready-made sanded sheets that you just chuck away when they become dirty.

That's about it. Remember: a big cage is better than a poky little one, and a solid one is the best; if the room is warm enough for you, it's warm enough for the birds; and, ideally, a budgie's best friend is another budgie. But if you do decide to keep one by itself, make sure it isn't lonely. Even if you don't set out to teach your pet to talk English, don't forget to talk to it. You never know. You might learn to speak Budgerigar.

Checklist

Advantages Budgies are cheap to keep and don't smell; they are cheerful and pretty to look at, and can be taught to talk.

Drawbacks They are generally noisy, and like all cage-birds, tend to scatter seed around the floor of the room.

Ailments	Constipation: give extra greenfood. Diarrhoea (usually caused by stale or sour food): cut out any greenfood; in a bad case the vet will give you sulphamethazine to treat the bird. Colds and chills: put the bird in a warm, even temperature. Add a few drops of rosehip-syrup to drinking water. Overgrown beaks and claws: you can deal with these yourself, but if you don't want to, take the bird to the vet. Sometimes there's a dry, extra length on the beak; clip it off, cutting away from the bird. Take care not to cut too deep, into the quick, when dealing with overgrown claws.
Sexing	Cocks: bluish or blue cere. Hens: pinkish or brown cere.
Suitable environment	Anywhere.
Lifespan	Five to six years if kept in a cage, but will live longer if allowed to exercise by flying round the room. Exceptionally, budgies can live as long as ten to twelve years.
Useful periodical	*Cage & Aviary Birds* (weekly).

2 Hamsters

Nowadays hamsters come in a lot of different colours, and there are millions and millions in the world. But as pets, hamsters are comparative newcomers. My old book didn't know anything about them, and that's not surprising, because it wasn't until 1930 that a zoologist found some in a deep burrow in the Syrian Desert and managed to rear three of them. All the millions of today's Golden hamsters are descended from those three.

It's no wonder they're so popular, because, to begin with, they look so attractive. They're nice and small – about six inches long when full grown – and seem to be a mixture of large mouse and little guinea-pig with a bit of teddy-bear thrown in. They're plump and sturdy and furry, and they have even less of a

Hamsters 13

tail than a bear, just a stub. But they make up for this by having some rather extraordinary and very useful things: cheek-pouches.

In each cheek a hamster has a fur-lined pouch that it can cram full of food till it looks as though it's got a bad go of mumps; then it toddles off home and empties the pouches into its larder by sweeping each forearm across its face.

Hamstern is German for 'hoarder', and that's what it does: stores up its food. It was very useful for the wild hamster, because it did away with the dangers of sitting about in the open to eat. It could just stock up with food in no time at all and then pop back into the safety of its burrow. And the pet hamster does the same.

In each cheek, the hamster has a fur-lined pouch, which it can cram full of food

Hamsters eat cereal grains. Any pet shop will sell you a good mixture. Besides that, give your hamster a bit of fruit (but don't leave it to go rotten) and some greenfood (but only a little). And there are quite a few odd things that hamsters are rather keen on, like porridge and bacon rinds and fish skin and eggs. I know one which is crazy about chopped almonds. And biscuits are very popular. The one thing all hamsters hate is an onion.

Always provide clean, fresh water in a drinking-bottle, though in fact individual drinking habits vary a great deal; some are always having a drink, and some only take a sip or two through the whole day.

Mind you, keep an eye on that larder the hamster will make to store its food, because although it'll accept everything you offer it, it won't necessarily be able to eat it all, and a lot will be wasted or go bad if you don't spring-clean its larder now and then.

As with so many other pets, you can buy very posh, expensive housing for your hamster, but it'll

Hamsters

be perfectly happy (and have more room) in an old drawer with a wire top over it. Remember, though, that hamsters are gnawing animals that can get through surprisingly small holes, and make sure that the hamster's house is built of hardwood, or face it with tin or wire to stop it chewing its way out.

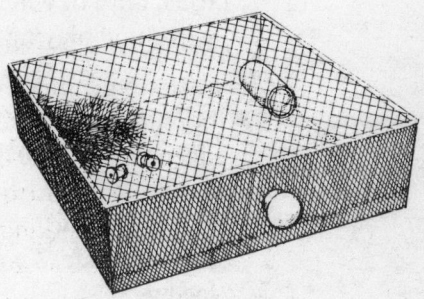

An old drawer with a wire top makes an ideal home for a hamster

Put clean sawdust on the floor, and for nesting material give it hay and some soft paper (not newspaper, because printing ink contains harmful substances).

And give it a lavatory. Hamsters use one corner as a rule, so if you put a big enough jam jar there, on its side, your hamster will do everything in it.

As for toys, I'm never too sure about wheels that they can get inside and trundle about; and please do avoid those transparent plastic globes they sell (the hamster is placed inside the globe and sealed up). These can only cause distress to the poor animal as it runs around trying to escape. I think I'd just stick to supplying cotton reels and the tubes from the inside of toilet rolls, both of which your hamster will enjoy playing with.

Also, remember that hamsters are nocturnal creatures that like to sleep most of the day, so put the house in a darkish corner. The animal will be most active in the early evening. That's the time to feed it.

One of the most important things is handling, and that's something you must get right straight away, otherwise you may end up with a bad-tempered pet that bites you, which is no kind of pet at all. Handling must be done slowly, deliberately, gently. When you first get your pet, show it your hand (not from above, that's a threat, but on its level) and stretch it slowly towards the animal. Close the fist because if your hamster should nip,

Hamsters 17

it won't hurt you much, whereas a bitten finger-tip does. Then, offer it food in your fingers. Next, begin to stroke it, talking to it, quietly. Once you've made friends, you can pick it up. When it's used to you, which it very soon will be, there won't be any problems.

When you first get your hamster, handle it slowly and deliberately. Show it your closed fist – not from above, but on the hamster's level

Remember one other thing, though, when you're carrying it around. Hamsters don't seem to have a clue about heights, perhaps because they're ground-dwelling animals, so if you've got it crawling about on your jersey or t-shirt, have your hands cupped ready to catch it if it decides to try a free fall. It won't land on its feet like a kitten would but most probably on its head.

You can teach your hamster simple tricks. One good one is to say its name and give it the command 'Stand' while you hold a titbit above its head. When it rises on its hind legs, it gets a reward. It will soon learn to stand whenever you hold your hand over its head. And it'll soon learn to come when it sees you, especially if you allow it some temporary freedom, say, to sit in your chair with you or walk about the carpet. These animals seem very much to enjoy such privileges, and one has heard of them lying down in front of the fire beside the dog!

You can teach your hamster to stand on its hind legs while you hold a titbit above its head

Hamsters

Hamsters don't live much beyond two years, so buy a young one. You can tell a young animal because the insides of its ears will be covered with tiny, white hairs. The insides of an adult's ears are bare. And look for a bright eye and sleek, soft fur and a solid, chunky feel to the animal when you pick it up. Don't ever consider one with runny eyes or nose, or one with patchy, mangy-looking fur; but don't worry if it has a mark like a spot on each hip – that's all right.

Finally, a very important word of warning. There are plenty of pets, most in fact, that will live contentedly together, and are happier with a companion of their own kind. But hamsters are solitary animals, and if you try to put two together, they will fight like tigers.

Unless, of course, you want to breed. Now this isn't a book about breeding pets, only about keeping them, but here's a story about breeding hamsters to show you the dangers. You should remember that hamsters breed throughout the year, that they can start as young as two and a half months, and that it only takes two weeks and two days after mating for the babies to be born.

A long time ago, I had a pair of Golden hamsters. I was a student at an agricultural college, living in a huge old house, three storeys high, with attics above and cellars below, a house filled with passages and cupboards and curious hidey-holes. And my hamsters chewed a hole in their box and escaped.

That happened in January. By the following Christmas there were hamsters everywhere. Walk down a passageway, open a cupboard, peep into a hidey-hole, and you were likely to see some of the hundreds of hamsters that now lived in that huge old house. Take my advice. Just keep one.

Checklist

Advantages A very good choice if you only want a single pet. The hamster is small, easy to carry about and enjoys being handled. It is clean in its habits and doesn't smell. Its pouching habits are unique and interesting.

Drawbacks The hamster is not very long-lived. It does tend to sleep a lot by day.

Ailments Colds: put the animal in a box the sides of which you've smeared with Vick vapour rub. Diarrhoea: keep on a totally dry diet. 'Wet tail': a nasty type of dysentery, where the fur round the anus is wet; a job for the vet. Pouch abscess: sometimes an animal will pouch something sharp that pierces the lining. It may have to be destroyed.

Sexing In the female, the genital and anal openings are very close together; in the male, a third of an inch apart. Also, the female's body is more tapered towards the rear.

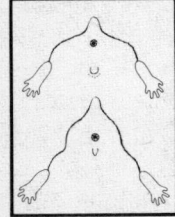

Male

Female

Suitable environment Anywhere.

Lifespan Not much over two years.

3 Cats

For some funny reason that I've never quite understood, people's feelings about cats are pretty sharply divided. Some love them above all other pets. Some simply can't stand them, perhaps because the cat is really just a miniature tiger and still, after thousands of years, makes them feel what early man must have felt when a sabre-tooth stuck its great head into the cave.

My father couldn't bear them. In fact, once, when my old ginger cat tactlessly jumped onto his lap, he said, 'Get off, Jinks! You *know* I don't like cats!' just as though she really did know. Jinks, incidentally, was a ginger cat who had once turned coal-black. When I first brought her home as a tiny kitten and put her down on the sitting-room floor, something frightened her and she shot straight up the chimney. It was summer, luckily, so there was no fire in the grate, but she was quite a different-coloured kitten by the time we got her down.

Siamese Seal-point

Colour is one of the attractions of cats, because they have it in such variety. Black ones (lucky if they cross your path but they must be travelling from right to left), white ones, gingers, tortoiseshells, tricolours, tabbies, blues, greys and creams; there's no end to the list. And the catalogue of different varieties is endless too: Shorthaired and Longhaired, Siamese and Burmese and Persian and Chinchilla and a whole lot more.

But you don't have to buy an expensive pedigree animal. An ordinary moggy makes just as good a pet and may indeed be more intelligent than a very well-bred one, some of which (Persians, for example) are not, I suspect, all that bright. And all kittens are equally delightful.

Blue Burmese

But before you fall for a pretty, playful, irresistible kitten, remember that it will grow into a cat that, with normal luck (if it makes use of all nine of its lives), will be with you for between twelve and sixteen years, or occasionally even more.

Cats are total carnivores. Meat is all they need. Milk is good for growing kittens, but adult cats don't require it. Water is all that's necessary by way of a drink, and owners who give saucers of milk (or even cream!) to full-grown cats are simply making them fat. And fat cats, like fat humans, are less healthy and don't live as long.

Chinchilla kitten

A kitten should have four small meals a day until it's about ten weeks old. Then you can gradually reduce the number of meals to two.

Cats are far too dignified and independent to obey orders like dogs, but, being naturally clean and tidy, they're easy to house-train. Choose a corner of the room (nowhere near the spot where you intend feeding the animal) and put down a tray, with sand or cat-litter in it, and the kitten will use it as a lavatory, burying everything neatly as all cats do. Mix a bit of earth in with the cat-litter, because this makes it easier for the kitten to learn the next step: to use the garden. And the best way to ensure that it can always get outside when

A kitten will quickly learn to use a tray filled with sand or cat-litter as a lavatory

it needs to is to have a cat-flap in your door. Mind you, it's perfectly possible for a cat to live the whole of its life without access to the outside world – in a high-rise flat, for example – but I'm not sure that sort of existence is altogether fair to the animal. If you *must* keep a cat indoors, it will need grass (a pot of cocksfoot) and a stropping-board (a bit of coconut matting tacked on a board). It is cruel for a former outdoor cat to be confined indoors, so start as you mean to go on.

As for somewhere to sleep, don't waste money on an expensive bed. Any old cardboard box will do just as well, with a bit of blanket in it.

A cat-flap

Don't continually pick up your kitten when it's asleep during the day – it needs its rest. And give it a small log of wood to sharpen its claws on, otherwise it may choose a table-leg or some other bit of nice polished furniture. Watch out for electric flexes: when you're not using an electrical appliance, switch it off and pull out the plug.

28 Pets for Keeps

An ordinary moggy makes just as good a pet as an expensive pedigree cat

Cats 29

Here are some other things to think about. Cats are usually very healthy animals, but one very infectious disease they can contract is cat 'flu. Get your kitten vaccinated against it.

It's a good idea to get your cat a log of wood on which it can sharpen its claws

Cat collars aren't a good idea. Cats climb trees, and collars can get caught on branches and hang their wearers.

Cats can get fleas: if you find clusters of tiny dark-brown granules in your cat's fur, dust it with *cat* (not *dog*) flea-powder. Groom (brush and comb) your cat regularly. And don't worry: cat fleas won't live on humans.

Lastly, something that it is very sensible to do when your kitten is old enough (and your vet will advise you on the right time) is to have it neutered. Otherwise there can be problems with full-grown cats. Males spend a lot of their time away from home looking for a mate, and fighting with like-minded tom-cats; and they also like to mark their territory (your house) which can make for wet, smelly chairs and curtains. Females come into season regularly and frequently, and then they are searching for mates, and very noisily too, yelling their heads off with lovesickness day and night (the Siamese, in particular, makes the most ghastly wailing noise, like a banshee). And cats do seem to like having kittens. We had one called Dulcie Maude, which had a hundred and four kittens in her lifetime. Neutering solves all these problems.

Whatever size, shape or colour of cat decides to do you the honour of adopting you, remember this: however long it condescends to live in your house and accept food and admiration from you, it will never belong to you in the way that a dog does, never worship you as a dog would.

You may think that your cat belongs to you. Your cat knows that you belong to it.

Checklist

Advantages — The cat can live anywhere, from farm to flat. It is long-lived, easy to keep and a beautiful, graceful animal (that also catches mice).

Drawbacks — Entire toms can be smelly, entire queens noisy. Cats can scratch furniture and material. A very few do remain dirty in the house.

Ailments — Two principal ones are Feline Infectious Enteritis (vaccination at twelve weeks and boosters later) and cat 'flu, which is a very infectious virus and once again should be guarded against by vaccination.

Sexing — It is very difficult to tell male and female kittens apart (though easy with adult cats). If you are not able to tell, ask a vet to check for you.

Male   Female

Suitable environment	More or less anywhere, but best if you have a garden.
Lifespan	Varies with the individual cat, but generally cats are long-lived, and there are plenty on record that have lived well over twenty years.
Useful periodicals	*Cat World* (monthly). *Cats* (weekly).

4 Guinea-pigs

Guinea-pigs really ought to be called 'Cavies'. That's the proper name that breeders and exhibitors use, but I'm going to stick to 'guinea-pig', which is what most people say. The history of this name business is quite simple.

As long as two thousand years ago, in South America, a creature called the Restless Cavy was being tamed and kept (for food). The descendants of these animals were imported into Europe about 1700; and, probably because they'd been shipped from Dutch Guiana and looked vaguely like tiny pigs, they were saddled with the name 'Guiana-pig', which later became 'guinea-pig'.

But there is one way in which the guinea-pig's ancestry makes it very different from most other rodents. The babies are born in a very advanced state, sixty-five to seventy days after mating, not blind, hairless and helpless like mice or rabbits, for example, but fully furred, with their eyes wide open and with a complete set of teeth. They're on the move immediately, just as the babies of the Restless Cavy had to be when born upon the open South American plains. And very soon after birth they are eating solid food.

Newborn guinea-pigs are fascinating little things, all heads and feet. (Incidentally, there are four toes on each front foot and, three on each back one.) But if you're planning to keep a couple (which is a better idea than having a solitary one — guinea-pigs, unlike hamsters, are very companionable and like to have a friend to chat to), keep two females, or sows as they're called. Two boars, unless they've always been together, say, as litter-brothers, will fight.

Guinea-pigs especially benefit from being handled. So do most pets, of course, but a guinea-pig, unlike a heavy rabbit, is just the right size for carrying about with you and

Guinea-pigs

will become very tame with handling.

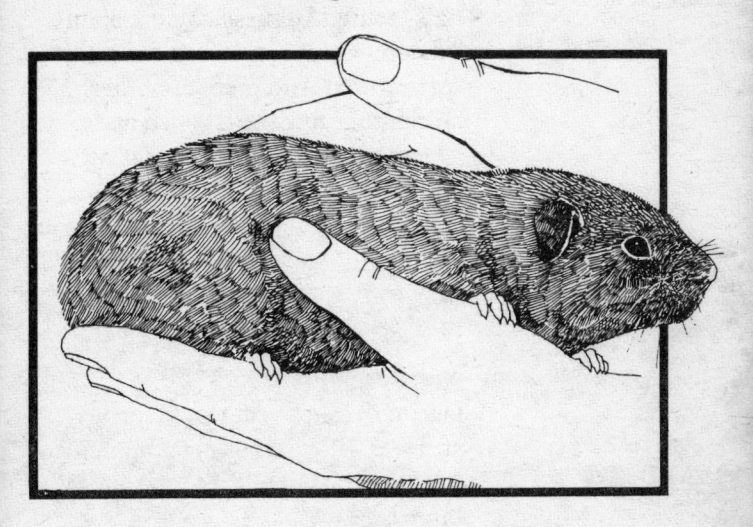

To pick up a guinea-pig, put one hand under its belly and the other over its back

To pick one up, put a hand under its belly (head towards you) and the other over its back. And remember that guinea-pigs are remarkably stupid about falling and seem always to land on their noses. Even a fall of no more than eight inches can be very nasty.

There are three main varieties of guinea-pig: the Smooth (which means what it says), the Abyssinian, which has rough hair sticking up in a series of rosettes, and the Peruvian, which has such a great deal of long, silky hair that it's sometimes hard to tell which way it's facing. All these come in many different colours and combinations of colours. And there are other kinds too, like the Crested and the Sheltie. My own favourite is the Abyssinian.

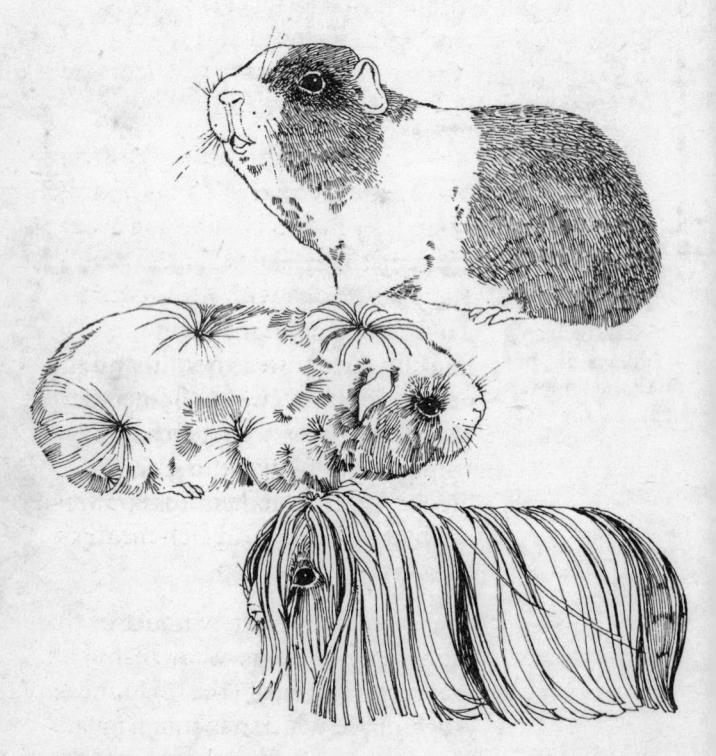

(*from top to bottom*)
the Smooth, Abyssinian and Peruvian guinea-pig

Some pet shops stock fairly typical specimens, but you just might end up with a rather long-nosed, ratty-looking animal. A good guinea-pig has a very distinctive shape: the body should be short and cobby, with broad shoulders and a short, broad, rounded, snub-nosed head, ears at right angles to the head and slightly drooping. It's best to buy from an experienced breeder.

Feeding is easy, because guinea-pigs love eating and aren't a bit fussy. In fact, they like to be nibbling away at something all day long. There's nothing wrong with the mixture you can buy, except that it's a boring way to feed, both for you and the animal, when there's so much pleasure to be gained (by you) and to be given (to the guinea-pig) by collecting supplies of wild greenstuff, or 'green meat' as it's sometimes called.

There's a huge variety of plants that are suitable, but perhaps best of all, and luckily one of the commonest, is the good old dandelion. Did you know that the dandelion, because of its jagged-toothed leaves, got its name from the French *dent de lion* — lion's tooth? There are loads of other plants that are enjoyed — I've listed some in the Checklist — and guinea-pigs like a whole lot of different vegetables like cabbage and cauliflower and carrots and swedes and beetroot as well.

Give them a bit of the ready-made mixture if you like, specially on cold winter days, but they do appreciate variety in their diet. And always provide them with some good meadow hay, because they need the fibre in it.

For bedding you can use some straw in very cold weather, but generally all that's needed on the hutch floor is sawdust. And don't forget to provide a water-bottle. Make sure it's properly attached to the side of the hutch with strong wire. Water, hay, greenfood, root vegetables — two feeds a day of these and no guinea-pig will complain. They *are* great complainers if things aren't just right (if supper's late, for example); you will find they are very vocal creatures with an extensive language that includes chatterings and chucklings and whistlings and a very loud squeal when they're hungry. Unlike the usually silent rabbit, the guinea-pig is extremely chatty.

A movable, wire guinea-pig run

Quite a good way to keep guinea-pigs in summertime is to make a movable wire run for them (with a shelter-box) and use them as lawn-mowers; they don't burrow, but if you're going to leave them out at night the run must have a wire bottom (of a large mesh so that they can graze through it) because a passing fox will soon dig its way under.

But generally, and certainly for the greater part of the year, what is wanted is a good, roomy hutch and I mean roomy. Some books will give you measurements for a hutch: two feet long, eighteen inches deep, ten inches high, that sort of thing, for one animal. Miles too small, I say. The important thing is that your pets should have plenty of space to potter about in; the bigger the better. Don't bother with a separate sleeping compartment, that's not necessary, but make sure you have small-mesh wire-netting on the front, because if there should be rats about, they are not good news for guinea-pigs.

I'm not too keen on outside hutches. It's difficult to protect the animals against the worst of wind and rain, let alone snow. Ideally, put your hutch in a shed or a garage, somewhere dry and draught-free, and your guinea-pig should have a happy life and, hopefully, quite a long one compared to some small animals. Most seem to survive five years or so, and one Crested sow that I had lived two years with me and then another eight with one of my daughters before she finally turned up her fourteen toes. Zen, she was called. People usually become grey-

and then white-haired as they age, but Zen darkened, from a pale gold to a mahogany colour.

I've always kept guinea-pigs, but not always sensibly. In our garden when I was a small boy there was a kind of miniature wood, a little spinney of half-grown Christmas trees and bramble bushes and rough grass, about the size of a tennis-court and surrounded by a low wire fence. I thought it would be fun to try to establish a colony of free-ranging guinea-pigs, and I turned out a dozen into this spinney and left them to get on with things.

At first all went well. They found all their own food, and by the middle of that summer the dozen had become three dozen. But then, gradually, the numbers seemed to grow less and less, and it became a job to find more than one or two in the tangle of vegetation. But somebody else was finding them all right. A bob-tailed black cat.

Be warned. Keep your guinea-pigs safe and snug. Black cats are only lucky for some.

Checklist

Advantages Guinea-pigs are very little trouble to keep, have no objectionable smell, are seldom ill, get extremely tame and are very conversational. They provide excellent manure for the garden.

Drawbacks None that I can think of, unless you want a silent pet.

Ailments Usually very healthy. Damp and draughty conditions may lead to colds. Poor-quality hay could contain fleas; dust against them. In older animals, claws may need clipping – not too far back or you will cut the quick and cause bleeding.

Sexing Gentle pressure either side of a boar's genitalia, which are roundish, will make the male organ extrude. The sow's organ is a slit. Do be very careful and very gentle when examining your pet to check what sex it is.

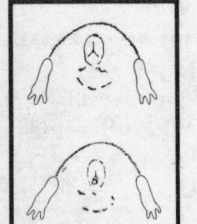

Female

Male

Guinea-pigs

Suitable environment	Guinea-pigs aren't house-pets. They need housing in a building. It helps to have a garden.
Lifespan	Quite long, say, five to eight years.
Wild plants suitable as food	Blackberry bramble; chickweed; clover; common comfrey; dandelion; field bindweed; grasses; groundsel; nettle (dried, makes good hay); common plantain; shepherd's purse; sow thistle; yarrow. (Many of these are illustrated on pages 44–5.)
Poisonous plants to avoid	*Take care never to feed any of the following plants or flowers, which are all poisonous, to your guinea-pig*: bluebell; buttercup; deadly nightshade; all evergreen shrubs and trees; foxglove; greater celandine; hyacinth; larkspur; poppy; snapdragon; snowdrop; tulip. Wild flowers, anyway, should never be picked. (Many of these are illustrated on pages 45–6.)

44 Pets for Keeps

Safe plants

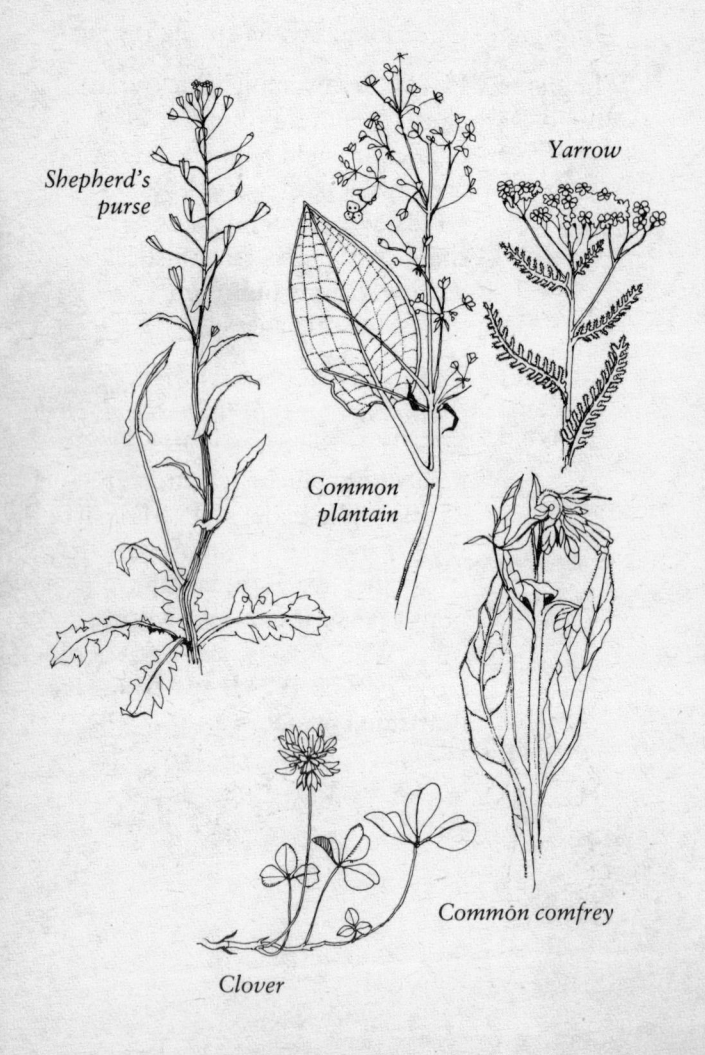

Shepherd's purse

Common plantain

Yarrow

Common comfrey

Clover

Guinea-pigs 45

Safe plants

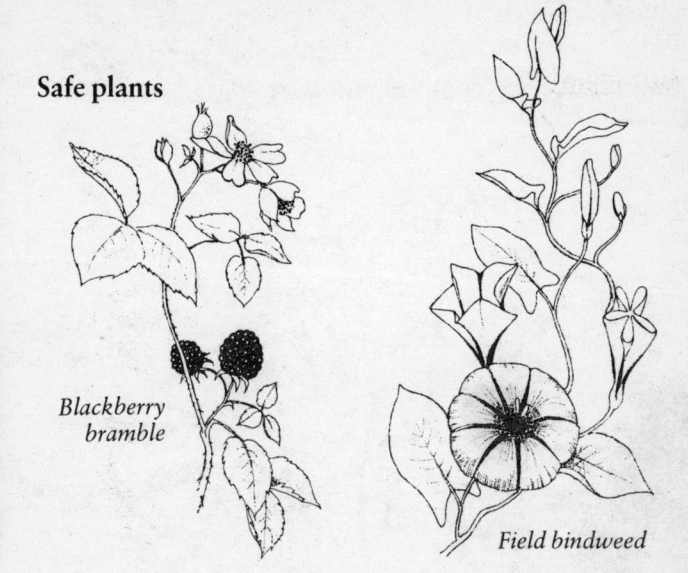

Blackberry bramble

Field bindweed

Some poisonous plants

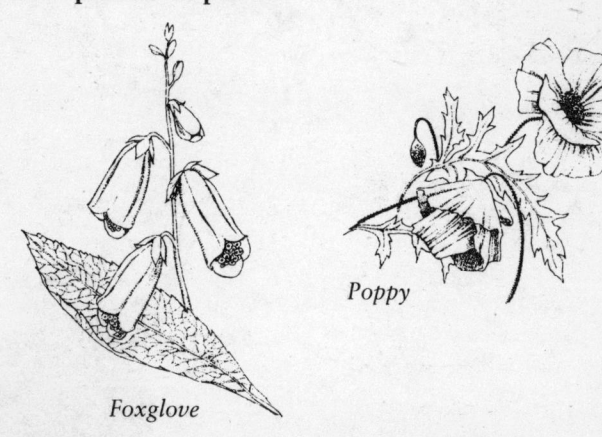

Foxglove

Poppy

46 Pets for Keeps

Some more poisonous plants to avoid

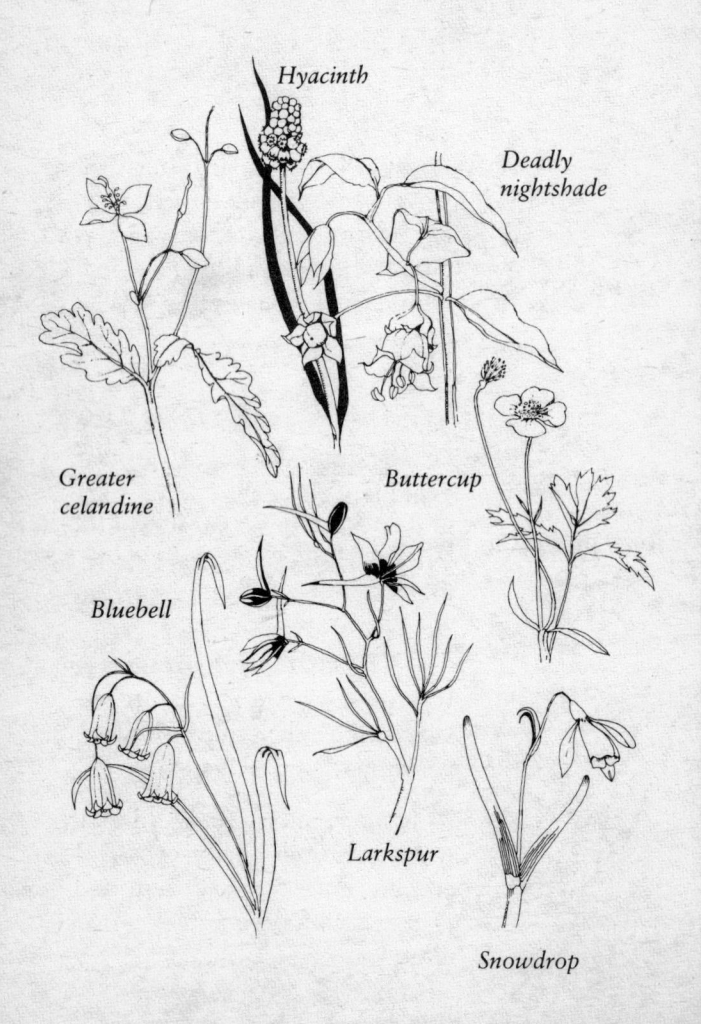

Hyacinth

Deadly nightshade

Greater celandine

Buttercup

Bluebell

Larkspur

Snowdrop

5 Mice

One of the attractive things about pet mice is their small size. Just because they're so tiny, you know as you watch them how a giant would feel if he lay down flat and got one eye to a window of your house.

And as well as being small, mice are very neat in their habits, forever grooming and tidying themselves and straightening their whiskers before scurrying off about their business, looking for some food or a drink, or doing a bit of nest-building, or just having a run round the cage to make sure everything's the same as it was yesterday.

Wild mice, of course, are all much the same rather boring brown colour, but there are dozens and dozens of different tame pet mice: white ones, black ones, chocolate-coloured or silver ones, mice of all shades of cream and red and fawn and soft lavender-blue, mice with special markings, and spots, and patches – there's no end to the choice. Some have black eyes, some pink. And perhaps quite a good kind for a beginner is what mouse-breeders call the PEW; that's not a hard bench that you sit on in church, but a pink-eyed white. For one thing, it looks so

White mouse

obviously different from a wild mouse, which is a good thing if you happen to live with anyone who screams and jumps on chairs at the sight of one of those. And, for another, the pink-eyed varieties, perhaps because their sight is not quite as good, seem calmer than some of their black-eyed cousins.

But whatever colour you choose, a mouse is a pet that's cheap to buy, cheap to feed, easy to keep, and a lot of fun to watch and handle.

The more you carry yours round with you, the tamer it will get. Slide your hand over its body and pick it up by the root of its tail, to put it on your other hand or your arm. I've seldom known one to bite.

House mouse

If you can, buy stock from a breeder, but if you do go to a pet shop, make sure the animals look healthy. Never buy a mouse whose fur looks patchy, whose eyes are runny, or especially whose nose sounds snuffly, and don't go for mice that are obviously either very young or rather old.

How many mice you keep is up to you, and it may be a temptation to get rather a lot just because they are small and inexpensive. But think carefully about this, unless you're planning to become a breeder. Mice can have young at a very early age and can have them often; and it only takes three weeks from mating for the babies to be born (and sometimes there are lots of them).

On the other hand, don't buy just a single mouse. Mice like company, and it will be lonely. I think the best thing to do is to buy two or three females, or *does* as they are called. That way you won't finish up like the Old Woman who lived in a Shoe.

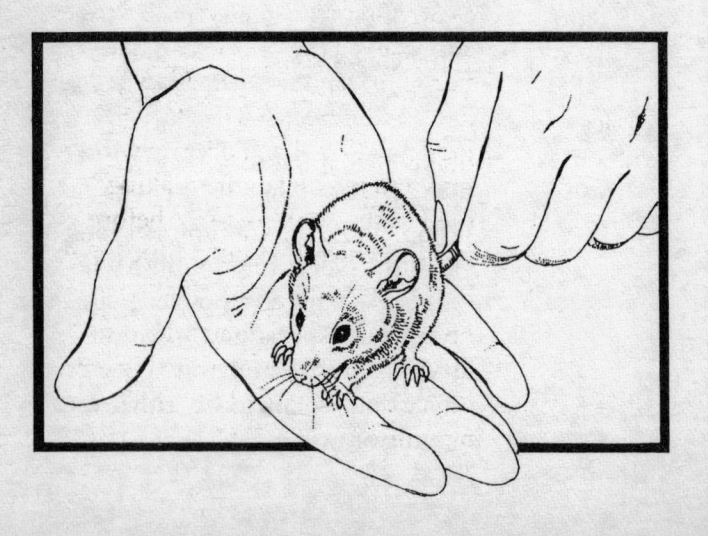

To pick up a mouse, slide your hand under its body and pick it up by the root of the tail

Mice

Choose does rather than bucks because the males have a slightly stronger scent.

Another advantage to this idea is that you could decide to keep animals of three contrasting colours, say, a PEW, a black-eyed Fawn and a Dove (which is a lovely greyish, bluish, pinkish colour, if you see what I mean). I used to buy my mice like this, from a mouse farm in Wales. Honestly, that's what it was called: 'The Mouse Farm'. I'm sure it's not there any longer, but you should be able to find a breeder who will offer you a choice.

As to housing, remember that although mice are small, they are very active, and they love having things to do (apart from eating), like climbing and swinging and jogging around and playing with toys and making and remaking their nests. So think twice before you buy the rather poky little boxes that some shops sell.

I used to make mine a real mouse-palace. Get a really big box, the size of a small rabbit hutch, and fit a sliding glass front on it so that you can watch everything that's going on. Make sure the box has grilles for ventilation and that it's not in a draught. Draught and damp are two things mice can't stand, apart from the cat. Then put in lots of ladders and walkways (just strips of wood an inch wide) at different levels, and perhaps a swing, and fit a nest-box, high up, so that they have to walk upstairs to bed like you do. The only other things you'll need are a couple of small pots, the kind you get fish- or meat-paste in, for food and water.

Mouse-palace

Once you've made your mouse-palace, you have to decide where to keep it. It's not a good idea to have it inside your own house; tame mice aren't totally non-smelly, and also they can sometimes attract wild mice. So keep it in a shed if you can or outbuilding or in the garage (on a shelf out of cat-reach). And just in case those wild cousins come visiting, store food in tins.

Finally, make sure the palace walls are thick enough, made of good hardwood or, if necessary, faced with tin inside; mice are great gnawers, and not only can they gnaw holes very quickly, they can squeeze themselves through what you would think were impossibly small ones.

I once had two mice, called Fairy Snow and Ogre Daz, that lived in a box-cage of thinnish plywood. One morning I found the cage empty, with a neat round hole cut in its side. Ogre Daz I never saw again; I'm afraid he came to a sticky end. A couple of weeks later I was rummaging in the shed where they had lived and where there were stored, amongst other bits of junk, some old toys: a broken scooter, an ancient cricket bat, some rusty Dinky cars, a discarded doll's pram. Something made me peer into the doll's pram, and there, in a fine nest made from the stuffing of the doll's coverlet and pillow, lay Fairy Snow with ten fat babies.

Mice like a great variety of foodstuffs. Just avoid giving them rich or strong food, like meat and particularly cheese. Mice have a distinctive smell, but it only becomes really unpleasant if you feed them stuff like that. Stick to bird-seed, any old bird-seed, they love that. You can also give them a pet shop mouse-mixture if you want to, but don't forget they like a whole lot of things that you eat: bits of bread, biscuits, breakfast cereal, a little slice of apple, a little bit of carrot — give tiny bits of everything. Don't feed more than they can clear up or you'll have a cage full of stale food, and that will attract wild mice. And make sure they always have clean water to drink, which means changing it often, because they love dunking things in it.

'Mice are smelly creatures', you'll hear people say. But if yours are, it's more likely to be your fault than theirs, because you're not doing your mouse-housework properly. Clean out every day. Scrape out all the droppings and put in fresh sawdust. And chuck away all their nesting material every so often and give them fresh. They'll much enjoy building it all up again. Bits of paper, dry leaves, pieces of old cloth, some hay or straw – they'll shred it all up and make a new nest and have a lot of fun doing it. And you'll have a lot of fun watching them.

Checklist

Advantages Even the largest mouse-palace doesn't take up very much room. Active and agile and multicoloured, pet mice are very interesting miniature pets that quickly adjust to being handled by their owners.

Drawbacks They're not particularly long-lived. They're apt to be smelly unless you take particular care. Their presence can attract wild mice to the area.

Ailments	Mice can't stand damp or draughts and can easily get colds and chills from bad conditions or from damp bedding. If you have a snuffly one, isolate it in a warm box, the sides of which you've smeared with some Vick vapour rub. Diarrhoea means you're giving too much sloppy food; stick to dry stuff.
Sexing	The female sex organ is close to the anus. The male organ is further away and shows as a blob.

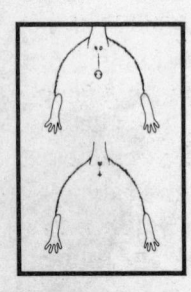

Male

Female

Suitable environment	Not for keeping in your bedroom. Put your mousery in a shed or outbuilding.
Lifespan	Two or three years.

6 Rabbits

It's not surprising that rabbits are such popular pets: they are very easy to keep; they don't smell or make a noise or a nuisance of themselves; they're easy to handle; and usually they are healthy and quite long-lived. And rabbits go very well with gardens (as long as you don't turn them loose) because there's a whole lot of vegetable matter – carrot tops and cabbage leaves are just two examples – that need never be wasted. The rabbit will make good use of it and in turn will give you some good manure that can be dug back into the garden to grow more carrots and cabbages.

Soft, furry, quiet and nice to look at, a rabbit makes a very good first pet; and what's more, a single one will live quite happily on its own, but (and it's a big 'but') it will need lots of attention from you. I don't mean just in the way of feeding it and cleaning it out, but of spending time with it and handling it. By the way, never pick up a rabbit by its ears or even by its scruff. The right method is to put one hand flat over its ears, pressing them down, and the other hand under its rump, and lift. Even if you don't actually want

To pick up a rabbit, put one hand flat over its ears and the other under its rump

to lift it, perhaps because you're too small and it's too big, give it lots of stroking. This does two things. It calms the animal and gives it confidence in you, and it grooms it, smoothing out moulty hairs and making the coat shine. And talk to it. All pets like to be talked to, even if, like the rabbit, they don't answer back. A rabbit that is simply stuck in a hutch at the bottom of the garden and has food shoved in twice a day, with no other kind of contact with you, is a prisoner, not a pet, and people who treat their animals like that are not proper pet-keepers. And a neglected rabbit can't even tell you when it is hungry, as a guinea-pig would by yelling.

Incidentally, one guinea-pig and one rabbit, if introduced when quite young, will live very happily together in the same hutch. They eat exactly the same sorts of food. And there are advantages to this arrangement. They're company for each other for one thing, and it doesn't matter which sex either is – you don't have to worry that you've been sold a male and a female and that you're going to come along one morning and find a nest of babies, as you might with two rabbits or two guinea-pigs.

If you have a big enough hutch and want to keep two rabbits of the same sex, they will have to be litter-brothers or litter-sisters. Put two strange bucks (or does) together and they'll fight like mad.

The spring is the best time to buy your rabbit, and go for a young one, say, eight to twelve weeks old. Then your pet will be with you a long time.

Rabbits tend to suffer more than most pets, I think, from being wrongly housed. They're hardy and uncomplaining and will probably survive in any old box with a bit of wire on the front, but that's no reason to condemn your pet to such an existence. I wouldn't mind betting that if I could go and look at a large number of individual pet rabbits, I'd have one criticism to make about nearly all of them: almost all the hutches would be too small. Rabbits have long hind legs and they like to stretch them.

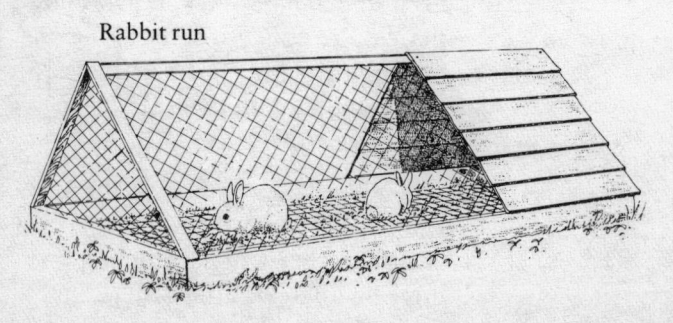

Rabbit run

Rabbits 61

As with guinea-pigs, it's possible, of course, in the good weather, to keep your rabbit in a run on grass, where it will have plenty of space to hop about; but make sure the run has a wire bottom — rabbits burrow.

But with regard to a hutch, start out by making certain that the one you provide is really roomy, and unless it's an outdoor hutch, don't divide it up to make a sleeping compartment: that just wastes space and isn't a bit necessary.

Rabbit hutch. A separate sleeping compartment is only necessary for an outdoor hutch

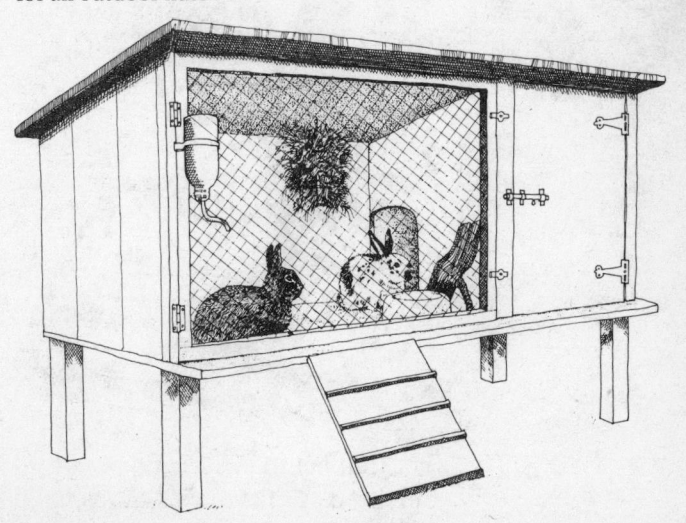

Some books will give you exact measurements (I usually double those), but all I'm saying is that it's easy to have too small a hutch but hard to have one that's too big. The size you decide on will depend on the rabbit you decide on, because there's a great variation in the choice of breeds, from Dwarfs to Giants. Just remember to be generous with space. And again, a hutch in a shed or a garage is far better than one outside in the cold and rain.

English rabbit

The number of different types of purebred rabbits makes choosing very exciting. Of course, you can simply go into a pet shop and buy a crossbred rabbit. I've nothing against pet shops – they'll sell you healthy stock as a rule; and I've nothing against mongrel rabbits – they'll make perfectly good pets. But there are so many fascinating purebred varieties – literally dozens, far too many to list here – and each one has its special attractions.

They vary tremendously in size, from the really big breeds like the Flemish Giant or the French Lop to tiny animals like the Netherland Dwarf with its round, snub-nosed head and short ears. They vary enormously in colour, as often their names tell you; Blue Beveren, New Zealand Red, Lilac, Silver, Smoke Pearl; and often there's a choice of colour within one breed, like the oddly named Silver Fox rabbit that boasts four distinct types of coat: black, blue, chocolate-coloured and lilac. And there are also the marked varieties, like the Dutch, which comes in half a dozen different colours but always has a white saddle, face markings and feet, and the English, which has chains of spots that are all supposed to be in a certain position.

Californian and Netherland Dwarf rabbit

Lastly, there are breeds of rabbits with most unusual coats. One example is the Angora, the only rabbit actually bred for its wool, which can grow to three inches long. The Angora doesn't have to be killed for its wool, any more than a sheep does. It is clipped, two or three times a year, and the wool is spun and made into lovely soft clothes like sweaters and scarves.

And another variety, the Rex rabbit, which has been developed in dozens of different colours, has a very short coat, with no stiff guard-hairs like normal rabbits, that is velvety-soft, like plush.

Feeding your rabbit can be very simple. You can do as the commercial breeders do: just give it manufactured rabbit pellets to eat and water to drink, and Bob's your uncle. If you do feed like that, one cupful of food per day is enough for a medium-sized animal. But, as with guinea-pigs, there's not much fun or interest for either of you in such a diet when there are so many wild plants; once again the old dandelion is best of all. The rabbit will also enjoy much garden and kitchen waste. Rabbits are herbivorous creatures and need roughage. As well as vegetables and greenstuff from the hedgerows, they very much like the prunings (they'll eat the bark) and the leaves of, amongst other trees, apple, pear, hazel and willow.

Variety is the spice of life for a hutched rabbit, and for a large part of the year, even if you live in a town, you can always find something to put in your 'green meat' bag. Be very careful, though, not to feed a lot of greenstuff if it's wet, because that will cause a nasty tummy upset. So will lawn-mowings if they've been left in a heap and allowed to heat up. A rabbit can't bring up its wind like many animals can, and eating a lot of wet greens can cause something called 'bloat', where gas is trapped in the intestines and death often results.

Lastly, always feed some good hay. Make a rack for it so that there'll be no waste. And stick to regular feeding-times, and don't make sudden changes in diet.

My own rabbit shed is rather well kitted out, I think. Each (big) hutch has a large water-bottle and a small but heavy (hard to tip over) feeding-pot. I use a scraper made from an old cut-down hoe for cleaning out, and there's a bin for sawdust and a cubbyhole for hay, mouse-proof tins for food, and a table to stand a rabbit on to groom it. Everything's shipshape and Bristol fashion.

One thing that might surprise you is to see your rabbit eating some of its own dung. Don't worry, that's perfectly normal. As well as the usual hard little droppings, every rabbit passes some that are softer that they eat direct from the anus. All rabbits must eat them in order to make their digestions work properly.

Rabbits, like people, are individuals with their own funny ways and their own likes and dislikes. I have a buck called Frank who is quite a character. Frank is a French Lop, a large breed with drooping ears, which is bred in several different colours, including what's called 'butterfly': white with brownish spots.

French Lop

But Frank is not just a large 'butterfly' French Lop: he's probably about the largest, and qualified for an entry in the *Guinness Book of Records*. He was one of a litter of only two babies, so he got a good start, and the last time I weighed him he was eighteen pounds. Yet he's not a particularly greedy rabbit, except for bread. He loves bread: a crust, or a slice that's got burnt in the toaster, or the fag-end of a stale loaf, Frank's not fussy about what kind of bread it is. The mere sight of it starts him grunting with excitement.

It's about the only time he gets worked up about anything, because there's one quality for which Frank should quite definitely be in the Guinness book. He's the laziest rabbit in the world, bar none. He doesn't just sit and rest like most rabbits. He lies flat out on his side, quite still, eyes tight shut, looking as though he were stone dead. Sometimes he even lies on his back. And he eats lying down. I've never known any animal that so much enjoys doing absolutely nothing.

Checklist

Advantages Rabbits are very easy to keep, to tame and to handle; they don't smell; they are seldom ill, usually silent, and long-lived. They provide useful manure.

Drawbacks Really, none that I can think of.

Ailments Many live long lives without illness. However, a few possible troubles are: diarrhoea; which can be successfully treated by feeding the rabbit blackberry leaves; and snuffles, which shows itself in the form of runny eyes and nose, sneezing and coughing. The vet will prescribe an antiobiotic for snuffles. Also, as I've said, bloat is a danger when too much wet greenfood is fed.

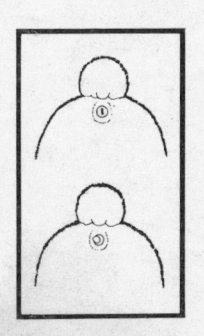

Sexing Very gentle pressure on either side of the sex organs will show the doe's organ as a slit, the buck's as a tip. In the mature buck the testes are visible. Be careful and very gentle when examining your rabbit to check what sex it is.

Female

Male

70 Pets for Keeps

Lifespan	Five or six years is common. I have known one lifespan of ten.
Wild plants suitable as food	As for guinea pigs: blackberry bramble; chickweed; clover; common comfrey; dandelion; field bindweed; grasses; groundsel; nettle (dried, makes good hay); common plantain; shepherd's purse; sow thistle; yarrow. (Many of these are illustrated on pages 44–5.)
Poisonous plants to avoid	*Take care never to feed your rabbit any of the following plants or flowers, which are all poisonous*: bluebell; buttercup; deadly nightshade; all evergreen shrubs and trees; foxglove; greater celandine; hyacinth; larkspur; poppy; snapdragon; snowdrop; tulip. Wild flowers, anyway, should never be picked. (Many of these are illustrated on pages 45–6.)

7 Gerbils

Gerbils are comparative newcomers to the world of pets. Once again my old book had nothing to say about them, because although the author must have known that they existed in many places – Mongolia, India, Israel, Egypt, Libya – he would have thought of them simply as wild animals.

That's certainly how I thought of them more than forty years ago when I used to watch them by the headlights of jeep or truck at night in the North African desert, and marvel at the distance that such small creatures could leap.

In action the gerbil is a fantastic jumper, like a miniature kangaroo. Its long hindlegs catapult it away, and its long tail acts as a balancer. It can even jump very high vertical distances from a standing start, which I'm not sure that kangaroos can.

So, once again, think generously about space when you decide upon housing for your gerbils. The size of cage you could buy or would make for a hamster is none too big, but don't forget that gerbils can squeeze through much smaller gaps. Be sure that the wire is of a small enough gauge to keep them in. And, talking of wire, if you decide to give your gerbils an exercise wheel, buy a solid plastic one without any bars.

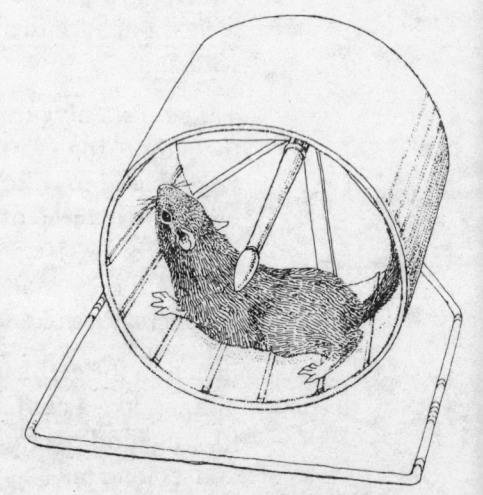

If you buy your gerbil an exercise wheel, make sure it's a solid one without any bars

Gerbils using wheels with wire struts have been known to cut their own tails off – something that

Gerbils

couldn't happen to a hamster! And gerbils are burrowers too, so it's a good idea to provide them with artificial burrows, like jam jars, in which they'll spend happy hours.

As to food, what's good for a hamster is good for a gerbil. Cereal grains are the gerbil's natural food, and any pet shop will sell you a suitable mixture. A tablespoonful a day is enough for one adult. Gerbils also fancy unsalted potato crisps, meal worms, dog-biscuits and hard-boiled eggs. Fruit and greenstuff are enjoyed, but remember, only tiny little bits are needed.

Once again, handling should be a gradual, gentle process until your newly acquired gerbils learn to trust you. Go slowly with that closed hand, talking all the while, and in no time you'll be able to pick them up. Always lift a gerbil by the root of its tail (never by the tip; this can cause awful damage), and then place it on your other hand.

The gerbil, like the hamster, does not smell. It is, however, much more wakeful by day, being by nature a very nosey beast. But the principal way in which the treatment of gerbils as pets differs from that of hamsters can be easily summed up: keep a hamster on his own, but gerbils hate to be alone. To be happy, a gerbil really does need a companion, and here's where the problems start if you're not careful.

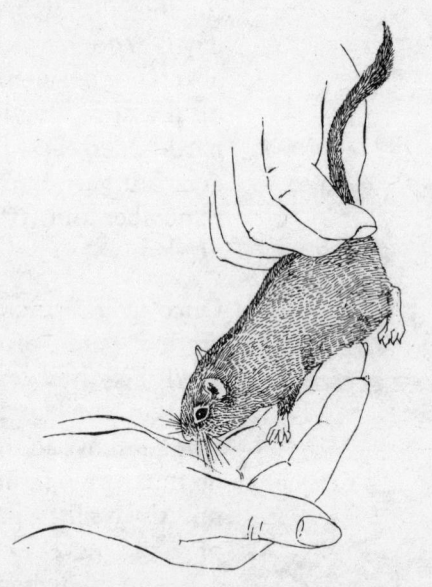

Always lift a gerbil by the root of its tail, never by the tip

Two gerbils of the same sex will live happily ever after, or rather for three or four years: that's their lifespan. A pair of gerbils, male and female, will live happily ever after too, but there won't be just two of them for long. It takes a mere twenty-four days from the time of mating for the female to produce a number (often a large number) of naked babies. And hardly will those babies have grown their hair before you must take them away from their mother — at twenty-one days of age — in time for the next lot to be born three days later. Worse, gerbils are sexually mature at three months. All of this, you can see, leads inevitably to a population explosion. And though you may be able to give one or two to your friends or sell half a dozen to a pet shop, you could very soon find that gerbil-keeping had become a nightmare.

Buy a couple from someone, preferably a breeder, who will make sure that you have two females or two males; always get them at the same time, for if you buy one and add another later they will fight for the territory. Or, better still, learn how to sex a gerbil yourself (see the Checklist). Then you'll only have yourself to blame if after a year you are the worried owner of over a hundred gerbils.

Now, gerbils are not only quick breeders. They're also quick movers, and when you're handling yours or cleaning them out, make sure you do it in a place where they can be recaptured. A friend of mine took her cage of gerbils out into the garden to clean it one sunny morning, and one of them escaped. It hopped away, much too fast for her to catch it, across the lawn and through the hedge. It was a female gerbil. And it was pregnant.

That was three years ago, and still her cat brings her the occasional dead gerbil and lays it thoughtfully on the mat. So far, the cat has caught twenty. Traces of nesting material and other signs show that the colony of gone-wild gerbils, all descendants of the one escaped female, has established itself in a deep, dry ditch that is all roofed over with a tangle of tree roots and undergrowth. But the strangest thing about this true story is that the gerbils that the cat now brings in are much bigger than usual – almost twice as big as normal. It looks as though only the largest and strongest have survived and that they in their turn have had bigger, stronger babies to face up to a life very different from that of their desert ancestors. The survival of the fittest seems to be operating at speed in a dry ditch beside a Wiltshire field. It's hard to believe that creatures can change that much – doubling in size – in three years, but gerbils can do a great deal in a very short time. If that one female had had (which is certainly possible) fifteen litters of, let's say, no more than six babies per litter for each of those three years, she'd have ended up with two hundred and seventy children. And imagine, if half of those two hundred and seventy had been females and each had had another ninety a year, and if half of all those nineties had been females, and . . . phew!

Two gerbils of the same sex will give you heaps of pleasure. Two gerbils of opposite sexes will give you plenty of worries: thousands and thousands and thousands of them.

Checklist

Advantages — Gerbils are cheap and interesting to observe; they don't smell and can become very tame.

Drawbacks — None really – unless you let them breed!

Ailments — Both colds and diarrhoea can be treated as for hamsters. Greasy fur can result from excessive humidity; don't wash it, the animal will groom itself clean. Something peculiar to gerbils is 'freezing' though no one's sure why. Sometimes, the gerbil will freeze when handled, forefeet stretched out, body quite still except for a trembling. It's possible that the reason is a hot hand; put the animal back in its cage.

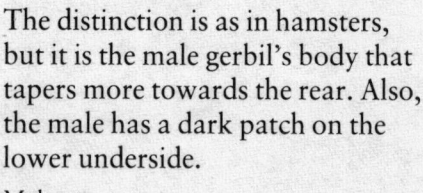

Sexing — The distinction is as in hamsters, but it is the male gerbil's body that tapers more towards the rear. Also, the male has a dark patch on the lower underside.

Male

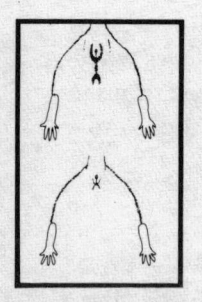

Female

Suitable environment	Anywhere. In your room, if allowed.
Lifespan	Three to four years.

8 Canaries

When I was small, I was sometimes taken to see a man who lived in a tiny cottage tucked under the shoulder of a hill. On one end of the cottage was a pig in a sty, and in the garden were lots of runs full of rabbits and two big hutches from which a number of ferrets stared hungrily at the rabbit runs with beady red eyes.

But the most thrilling thing for me was an open-fronted shed round at the back of the cottage, because inside it, against its three walls, were fixed dozens of bird cages, each containing a single canary. Some of the birds were tall and slim, some short and plump, some had strange topknots of feathers like little hats, but every one of them, it seemed, was always singing.

I know now that each was singing not just, as it seemed to me then, out of happiness, but to proclaim its territory. And what a miserable territory it was, a little wooden cage no bigger than a shoe-box, with a single perch in it the size of a pencil.

Take care that before you buy your canary you have a really comfortable cage ready for it. Canaries have been bred in captivity for a very long time and there is no instinct left to live the free life of their ancestors in the Canary Isles, so it doesn't seem wrong to me to cage them — as it would in the case of a Bullfinch or a Goldfinch or a Linnet — provided they have a suitable home.

You can buy all kinds of cages, of wire and plastic, or wire and metal, cages to hang up or to put on floor-stands, in dozens of different colours and designs, some of them very elaborate. But I think the best cage of all for a canary is a box-cage, a roomy one, long enough for the bird to do a bit of flying; principally because it is so much cosier, being proof against draughts, which canaries hate.

It should have two perches running from the wire front to the cage back and a cross-perch that goes the length of the cage. Fit the cross-perch a couple of inches away from the wire and just below the seed-hopper and the water-vessel, making sure each perch is at least half an inch wide. Pencil-width perches don't allow the bird to stretch its feet properly, and lead to cramp and broken nails. Natural twigs of the right size will do fine. And wherever you place the box-cage (never, incidentally, in full sunlight), make sure that the window-sill or the shelf is out of cat-jump. That's why my old friend had his fixed high on the shed walls. He was right to choose box-cages but, of course, very wrong to have such small ones.

There are loads of different types of canaries — the Border Fancy, the Roller, the Norwich, the Lizard, the Yorkshire, and lots more — but the whole object of choosing a single canary as a pet is for the pleasure of hearing it sing, and the cock birds are the songsters. Telling the sexes apart is tricky unless you're an

Canaries 83

expert, so listen before you buy.
Look also for a healthy bird,
bright-eyed, tight-feathered, and

Yorkshire (*left*)
and Border Fancy
canary (*right*)

active, hopping about briskly. An
indication of age is that a first-year
bird has white flight feathers on the
wings, and smooth legs and feet.
With age the flights become yellow
and the legs more scaly.

Canaries love variety in their food. The best basic mixture is two parts of canary seed to one part of summer rape. Egg-food is very good for them – you can buy this ready made – and they like coarse, dry oatmeal and crushed, sweet biscuit. Other favourites are finely scraped raw carrot, a tiny bit of apple, and greenfood (but never too much or too wet or frosted). As with so many pets, dandelion's the best; pick out just a couple of leaves from the heart of the plant; and they'll spend hours messing about with flowering grasses. Cuttlefish helps digestion and keeps the beak in trim, and they need grit.

Canaries love bathing!

One thing canaries do like is bathing, especially on warm days.

Canaries

You can buy a 'hang-on' bath that fits over the door opening, and bath-time should be early in the day so that bird and cage are properly dry before evening.

Generally, it's best not to handle a canary, but if you have to catch your bird, don't flap your hand about and panic it, but make a quick, decisive grab; and then lay the canary in the palm of your hand, with a thumb, very gently of course, across its neck.

The canary should be held in the palm of your hand, with a thumb very gently across its neck

One reason you might need to do this is to cut its claws if they grow over-long. Use a pair of sharp nail scissors and don't cut into the vein (you can see a red streak in each claw if you hold it up against the light).

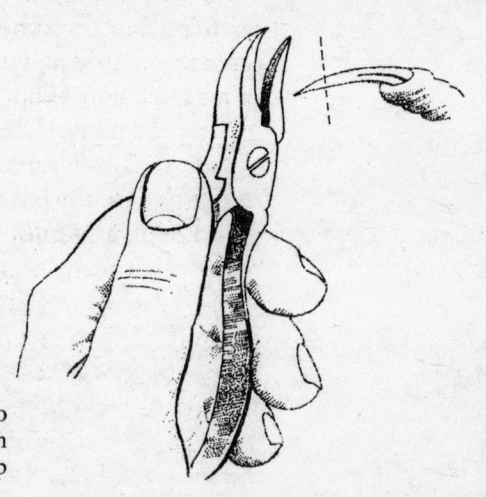

Take care not to cut overgrown claws too deep

Canaries are pretty healthy animals and suffer from very few diseases, but one problem that sometimes occurs is an infestation of parasites called Red Mite. Have a look at the Checklist to see how to deal with it.

Moulting is something that happens once a year, usually after mid-July. It takes several weeks, and during the time that the bird is dropping feathers it's a good idea to feed a bit extra in the way of greenfood and also a bit of bread sopped in milk. And three baths a week help.

You can't change the colour of your rabbit's hair or turn your guinea-pig into a punk, but you can alter the look of your canary. If it's a yellow variety, like a Yorkshire or a Norwich, you can change its colouring to a rich orange. If it's one of the buff-coloured types, you can change it to a shade of peach. This is done by what's called 'colour-feeding': giving the canary a special mixture of egg-food and a sweet Spanish red pepper, which you can buy made-up. Half a teaspoonful a day for fourteen days and then one teaspoonful a day is the dose, beginning in early July, before the bird starts to drop its first feathers, and then continuing right through the moult, say, for ten weeks in all. No good trying it on your budgie – it won't work.

If you're lucky enough (like me) to live in the country where you can hear any number of wild birds singing, then maybe a canary is not the pet for you. But in a town flat this bird makes a super companion. It's always busy, always cheerful, and it's difficult to feel miserable when you hear it singing away as though every day was the first day of spring.

But you've got your part to play too. Although the canary is one pet that is usually kept (and is happy to be kept) on its own, it needs plenty of attention and affection from you to live a full life. It seems to like to be one of the family, so don't forget to talk to it. Even if you'll never be able to sing like it can.

Checklist

Advantages — The canary is happy by itself, doesn't smell, and sings beautifully.

Drawbacks — All caged birds can scatter seed around the floor. Put a newspaper under its box-cage.

Ailments — Loose droppings are usually caused by improper feeding or overfeeding. Put it on the plainest food and add to its water something called Genuine Bird Tonic. Colds are usually caused by draughty

Canaries

conditions. If you think the unwelcome visitors called Red Mite are about and want to test for them, remove the perches and tap them on the edge of a bowl of water to see if any little red insects fall in. You can spray against Red Mite with a patent preparation, and dipping the ends of the perches in paraffin will clobber them.

Sexing Cocks seem to be a bit bolder and more richly coloured, and have slightly flatter heads. Song's the best bet: if it sings, it's male.

Suitable environment Any room, anywhere – so long as it's not cold, damp or draughty.

Lifespan Five to six years if kept in a cage, but will live longer if allowed to exercise by flying round the room. In exceptional cases canaries have been known to live as long as ten to twelve years.

Useful periodical *Cage & Aviary Birds* (weekly).

9 Bantams

The kind of pet you are able to keep obviously depends on where you live. A canary or a budgie would be perfectly happy in a town flat or a tower block, but to keep poultry you really have to have a garden, with room enough for a fowl-house and pen. Even then, ordinary, full-sized hens need quite a lot of space, which is why bantams make such good pets.

Bantams are miniature fowls. The average farmyard hen is not the cleverest creature in the world, but bantams, perhaps because they are so small and neat and quick in their movements, give the impression of being quite bright little birds. Certainly I suspect they are more intelligent than people give them credit for, and if they are kindly and gently treated and talked to (as all pets should be) will become very tame and show quite a lot of character.

If you're lucky enough to have a walled or securely fenced garden, it's possible to give them the run of the place, but that does present problems. Scratching up newly sown seeds or having a dust-bath in the flower-beds or pecking young plants to pieces is not going to make them (or you) very popular with whoever is the gardener in your family, so it's really best to

Inside a bantam-house

keep them in a wire pen. It must, of course, have a house attached, in which they can be shut at night to protect them from the weather and from foxes. Foxes used to be thought of as animals of the open countryside, but now every city and town has its fox population, and your bantams wouldn't last long if you just let them perch wherever they fancied for the night.

Mind you, if your wire pen is roofed over, they'd be perfectly safe if you forgot to shut them up, but they need shelter from cold and wind and rain. But if the pen has no roof, you must remember to pinion your birds or they will fly up out of

To pinion a bantam, cut back the big flight feathers on one wing only

it. Pinioning means cutting back the big flight feathers on one wing (with a pair of scissors – it's easy and doesn't hurt the birds) so that their flying action becomes lop-sided and they can't take off. Don't clip both wings, or they'll still be balanced and able to flutter up.

If you're just going to keep a few bantams, the house doesn't need to be very big. In fact, the smaller the cosier, provided it's properly ventilated, and that there's enough space for the birds to do two things in comfort: to perch contentedly in it at night, off the floor and with enough head-room, and to lay their eggs in it by day.

So you'll need a perch (two inches by one inch) long enough for all to roost, and a box or a couple of boxes (old apple-boxes will do) filled with straw. Two boxes to every five hens is about right.

Unlike some pets that may give you pleasure to look at or to play with but not much else, bantams will pay you back. You provide the food and they'll provide the eggs – and very good eggs they are, smaller, of course, than ordinary hens' eggs but very tasty. And it's great fun collecting them. 'How many today?' you'll come to think.

The only other equipment you'll need, in the outside run, is for food and water. A proper, galvanized drinking-fountain is best, because if you put a bowl of water down, the starlings and sparrows will use it to bathe in and make it mucky. And

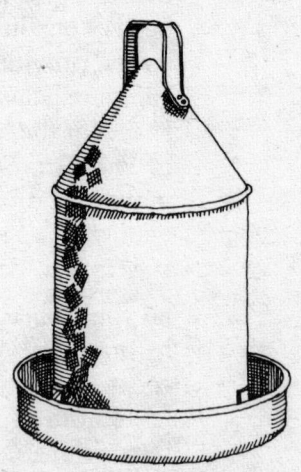

Galvanized drinking-fountain

you must think about those robbers when you're feeding. Use a metal trough – it'll last longer than a wooden one and is easier to keep clean – and don't feed ad lib unless you want a lot of it to go into the sparrows' crops instead of the bantams'. A roofed run, of very small-gauge wire, will, of course, keep the pesky things out.

The best times to feed are early in the morning, when the birds are first let out, and in the evening, so that they go to bed full. Any food that's suitable for ordinary hens is fine for bantams, though fortunately you need to provide much less of it. You could just feed layers' pellets, but another way, which they seem to enjoy more, is to feed a mash (layers' mash, wetted – with hot water in bitter weather – and made into a mixture that's just nice and crumbly, not sticky; it's not as easy for the wild birds to steal). Feed that in the morning and corn in the evening. And don't forget to provide grit, which any pet shop will sell, because bantams, like all birds, need it for digestion and for making shell for their eggs. A little box full, inside the house, will last a long time. Oh, and remember to unfreeze the drinking-fountain in really bitter weather. Finally, clean out all the droppings from the inside of the house once a week, and put fresh sawdust on the floor. You'll soon have a nice little heap of manure for the garden.

Only trial and error will show you whether your bantams are good layers — some strains are more productive than others — and are giving you as many eggs as you want. But three or four pullets is probably a good number with which to start. Never keep a single bird, which would be miserable by itself.

The other thing you have to decide is whether to keep a cockerel or no. One popular way of beginning is to buy a trio (a cockerel and two pullets), and then you can always add more pullets if you aren't getting enough eggs for the family. There is a disadvantage to keeping a cockerel. He's liable to start shouting that the new day has begun and wake you up a lot earlier than you'd like. But he does have certain advantages too. To begin with, bantam cockerels are very attractive birds. Often their colouring seems much brighter than that of the hens, and they have larger combs and long, flowing tail plumes. They're very proud-looking little beasts ('cocky' is just the word to describe them) and many of them, especially those bred originally from game birds, are as tough as nails. Once I had an Old English Game bantam cock called Prince Charming, because he obviously thought the world of himself and was for ever showing off in front of his hens. One day he picked a quarrel with a huge farmyard rooster about five times his size and weight. It was a fight to the death, but it wasn't Prince Charming who died.

Barred Plymouth Rock bantam cock

The other point about having a cockerel is that, by mating with his hens, he makes their eggs fertile.

Now this book is not about breeding pets, and keeping a cockerel with your bantam hens doesn't commit you to hatching out baby chicks. Just keep picking up every egg that's laid, and then when one of your hens goes broody (refusing to get off the nest, fluffing up her feathers and squawking and swearing at you), well, there's nothing she can do about it without any eggs to sit on. But because it's so easy and such fun, I can't resist telling you what to do if you should decide to let a broody bantam hen hatch a clutch.

First of all, don't just leave some eggs in the nest-box and allow her to sit on a heap of them. When you have a bird showing signs of going broody, start selecting a number of freshly laid eggs; check them, making sure they are a good shape and that there are no cracked ones; store them, narrow end down, at room temperature, till you have collected nine or ten, which is about the right number.

Now make a separate broody-coop – a box with a slatted front that she can't get out of on her own – and make a basin-shaped nest of straw in it. Then put the broody bantam in for two days on a couple of pot eggs (these are false eggs that you can buy, so that if the bird changes her mind and decides not to stay broody after all, nothing's wasted).

Broody coop

Then, when you're sure she's sitting tight, reach under the hen and swap the pot eggs for the ones you've collected. Dusk is the best time to do it. They'll take twenty-one days to hatch.

During that time, you must take the bird off the eggs once each day (evening is best – she'll settle back quicker) and put her down somewhere away from the coop with food and water for ten minutes or so, before letting her back on to the nest. Also, from the eighteenth day onwards, splash the eggs, while she's off feeding, with a little warm water; this will help with hatching. And because sitting still in one place for three weeks attracts parasites to a bird, dust her backside with insect powder at the start of the sit. Once the chicks are hatched, she'll do all the looking after. All you have to do is to provide them with chick crumbs for the first three to four weeks of their lives.

There's a huge choice of varieties of pet bantams. You may be happy just to have mongrel ones, but there are more than two dozen miniature versions of well-known breeds like Rhode Island Reds and Buff Rocks and Light Sussex, as well as the Old English Game (my personal favourites, which come in many different colours). And there are the Silkies, slightly bigger birds with feathery legs and top-knots — very good mothers.

Bantams

You can't expect bantams to lay anything like as many eggs as a full-sized commercial hen would. But you can expect them to give you a lot of fun – and to pay for their keep. You give them their breakfast. They'll give you yours.

Rhode Island Red bantam hen (*left*) and Old English Game bantam cock (*right*)

Checklist

Advantages	Bantams lay eggs, look pretty, are very little trouble to keep, and provide good manure.
Drawbacks	You have to remember to shut them up at night. And cockerels can be noisy in the early morning.
Ailments	Very few. Watch out for parasites.
Sexing	Cockerel has larger comb, longer tail feathers, different body shape and crows.
Suitable environment	You must have a garden, or at any rate sufficient space.
Lifespan	Seven or eight years, or more.
Useful periodical	*Poultry World* (weekly).

10 Rats

Just mention the word 'rat' and a lot of people will say, 'Ugh!' To call someone a 'dirty rat' means that you despise, even hate, and perhaps fear that person. All of which would be bad news for the pet rat if it were exactly like its wild cousin. But it isn't.

Rats in the wild live in colonies, as big as the food allows, and where it is plentiful, as on a farm, they can be a menace. Most farmers will tell you that the only good rat is a dead rat. But to have a tame rat of your own as a pet is a very different matter.

Tame rats have been specially bred for a long time. They are slightly smaller than the wild Brown rat, and come in different colours, the best known of which is the Albino, a white animal with pink eyes. There are also Fawn rats, and

Japanese Hooded rats (white, but with head, shoulders and saddle – a stripe down the spine – of black or any other distinct colour) and Capped rats (white, with a black or other-coloured head). And there's the Irish Black rat, which is black all over except for four white feet and a white triangle on its chest.

But, colour apart, the real surprise about the tame rat is its character. Not only is it very clean and not a bit vicious, but it's also extremely bright. The wild rat has every man's

Tame rats are clean, very intelligent and can be a lot of fun to keep

hand against it, but the tame rat has been specially bred by man, as a pet, and to be used, because of its intelligence, in all sorts of experiments to help us understand animal behaviour, and learning in particular.

That's the really interesting thing about keeping a rat: that it's a very knowing creature. This is why rats are such successful animals in the wild – because they use their brains. And your pet rat is a very brainy beast, as one look at its face will tell you. This makes it a lot of fun to keep, because, specially if you're inventive or mechanically minded, you can devise all sorts of games to amuse and interest both you and your pet.

Rats will learn very quickly to solve problems you may set them. They can be simple problems: you could build a kind of maze that a rat has to find its way through, to get to its food. Or simple experiments, like putting the same sort of food into a number of dishes of different colours, to see which colour is the rat's favourite. Or it's possible, if you're clever enough, to set them more difficult tasks. For example, you could fix up a contraption worked from an exercise wheel — on the same principle as the business of drawing water from a well — where the food could be lowered by pulley when the animal turned the wheel. Or you could even construct a series of boxes, differently coloured or marked with different symbols, only one of which actually contained food; you would find that the rat quickly learned the right one to pick and thus be rewarded for its cleverness. And always, you note, the reward is food.

Rats, wild or tame, eat absolutely anything, but if you're to keep your pet healthy, stick to a simple diet. For example, wholemeal bread is as good for your rat as it is for you. You won't want to eat it stale but that's how it's best for the rat; soak it in water — add a drop of milk if you like — and then squeeze all the moisture out of it before you offer it. Whole oats are good, and so are a lot of the things that suit other small rodents, like breakfast cereal or hamster-mixture or bird-seed. Nuts, and hard dog-biscuits in particular, give the rat's teeth lots of exercise.

Vary the diet occasionally by adding small quantities of fruit or vegetables or wild greenstuff, but steer clear of meat or cheese or anything rich. And, of course, always make sure that the animal has clean water in a drinking-bottle. One last word about food. Store it in vermin-proof containers. Otherwise you will have unwelcome visitors. As with pet mice, your rats will attract their wild relations if you leave food about where they can get at it.

The usual rules apply to housing your rat. Make sure that whatever cage you buy or build is plenty big enough. Room is needed not just for the animal to exercise itself, but for things you will want to provide for its interest and entertainment, like wheels and ladders and bits of twigs and cotton reels and all kinds of toys. They all give the intelligent rat something to do and to think about, something to stop it becoming bored. Just take care that none of them are painted or have plastic in them or sharp edges.

Be certain that the cage is escape-proof – rats are great gnawers – and, of course, put it in a not-too-cold, dry, draughtless place. And keep it clean. Rats do have their own peculiar scent, but if

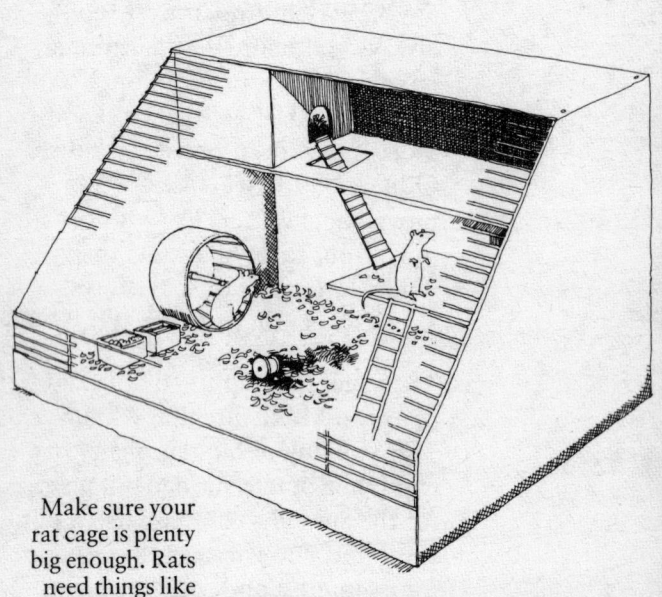

Make sure your rat cage is plenty big enough. Rats need things like wheels, ladders and cotton reels to keep themselves occupied

you keep their quarters really spotless, you'll find they're not at all offensively smelly. They tend to use one spot as a lavatory, and it's the work of a moment to clean this out every day with a sharp scraper and put in fresh sawdust. And, as with mice and hamsters and gerbils, they'll chop up whatever material you give them to make themselves cosy nests.

Buying a pair of rats – a buck and a doe – is probably not a good idea, as I once found out when I bought a pair of Hooded rats. For some reason that I've forgotten, I named them after an Indian god and his wife: Shiv and Parvati. And before long I had a great many rats.

Shiv was a very good father (buck rats are; if left with the doe when the babies are born, they'll be as nice as pie to their kids and help look after them) and Parvati was a very good mother. First, she had twelve babies. Later, she had fourteen. Later still (not all that much later), she had sixteen. You see the problem.

When you reckon that rats can breed at about three months of age and take only just over three weeks to produce their litters, you can work out, if you're good at maths, that Parvati could have given birth to well over a hundred babies in a year, and that if all the female descendants had chipped in and played their part, old Shiv would very soon have been the ancestor of literally millions of Hooded rats.

So I think I'd advise you to start with just one rat. But don't start at all unless you're prepared to work at your side of the relationship, which such a smart animal needs to be happy. And handling your rat is the most important part of that.

First, get your new pet accustomed to your scent and your voice. Then introduce it to your hand, very gently offering nice little bits of food, because a big, suddenly grabbing hand is a threatening thing and a bite from a rat is a different matter from a mouse's

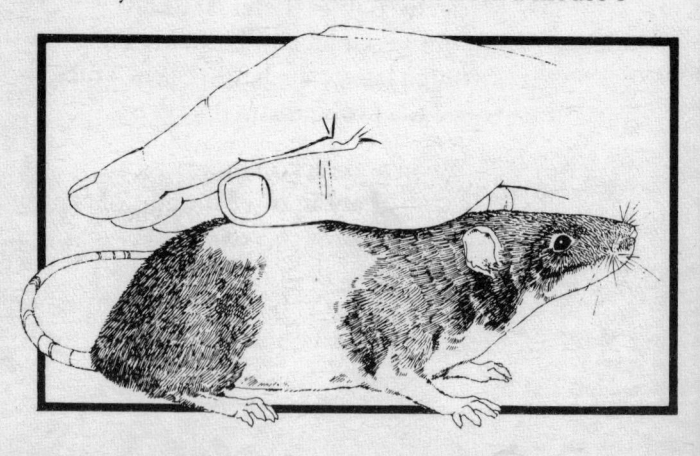

To pick up a rat, place your hand over its body with your fingers towards its tail and its nose under your wrist

nip. Once the rat is used to taking food from your fingers, you can pick it up. There's only one right way to do this: never pick it up by its tail alone or by the scruff of its neck, but place your hand over its body with your fingers towards its tail and its nose under your wrist. Then you can put it on to your other, open hand, and a firm grip of the base of its tail will stop it jumping off, until it's used to you. Which it very soon will be as it gets to know and trust you.

That's the rewarding thing about a tame rat. As well as being intelligent and clean and gentle, it seems able to become really fond of its owner.

Parvati died of a chill before she could produce her fourth litter (which I suppose might have been of eighteen babies, the way she was going), but old Shiv lived a long time and used to go everywhere with me, sitting on my shoulder. I can still recall the tickle of his whiskers on my neck.

Checklist

Advantages — Rats are intelligent, gentle and can form a bond with their owners.

Drawbacks — They may attract wild rats. Also some people might not like their slightly sweetish scent.

Ailments — Like mice, rats should not be kept in damp or draughty places, as they can easily catch colds and chills. A snuffly rat should be isolated in a warm box, the sides of which you've smeared with some Vick vapour rub. Diarrhoea means you're giving it too much sloppy food – stick to dry stuff.

Sexing — The female sex organ is close to the anus. The male organ is further away and shows as a blob.

Male

Female

Suitable environment — Not for keeping in your house. You need a shed or other outbuilding in which to keep the cage.

Lifespan — Five or six years, or more.

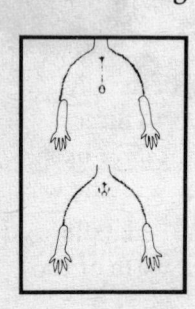

11 Goldfish

Usually, choosing an animal is something you've thought about and planned for. It should be, anyway. But one pet that it's possible to acquire quite unexpectedly is a goldfish, for goldfish are often offered as prizes at fêtes or fairs.

If you should win one like this, there's a simple rule. Don't accept it unless you're prepared to look after it. I dread to think how many small goldfish have been brought home in a plastic bag, dumped in some quite unsuitable container, and expected to live and thrive. Mostly, I suspect, they die – of shock at being plunged into water that's too warm or too cold, or of oxygen starvation, either because the container hasn't enough surface air space or because too much food of the wrong sort is dropped in and left to rot and poison the water.

As with many other pets, the best way to go about goldfish-owning is to buy from a good pet shop. Choose fish that look healthy, which means that they are swimming around actively, using all their fins, and that the dorsal (back) fin is upright. And choose smallish fish: they will probably be younger and therefore have a longer life with you, and it is easier, for example, in a six-gallon tank, to keep two three-inch fish healthy than one six-inch fish. Try anyway to keep at least two fish together, because goldfish are companionable creatures that naturally swim in schools.

But before you buy your fish, you must have their home ready. Don't use the old-fashioned goldfish bowl. Why such a thing was ever designed I don't know — perhaps in an attempt to stop cats from scooping the fish out — but the shape of it means that there is nothing like enough area of water exposed to the air to provide the oxygen the fish need.

Buy a proper glass aquarium tank (a plastic one will do to start with

Goldfish 115

for just a couple of little fish) and always err on the side of giving the fish what may seem to be too much space.

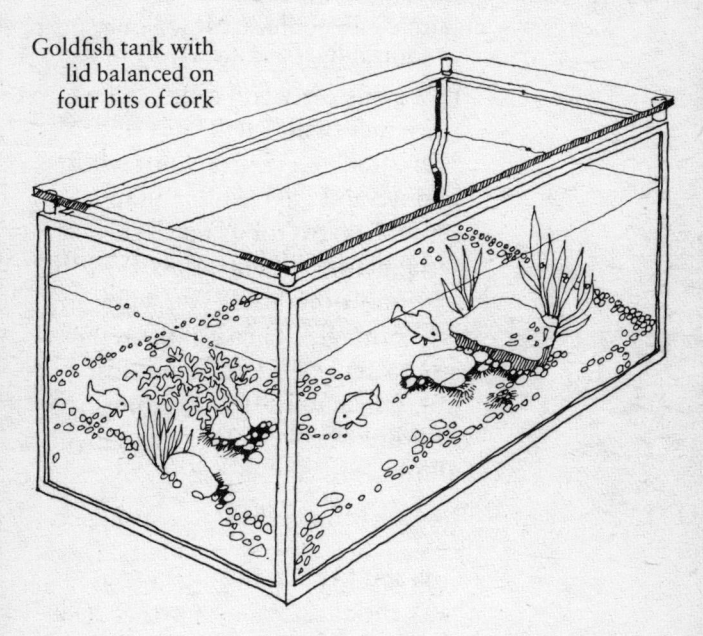

Goldfish tank with lid balanced on four bits of cork

Long before you buy your fish, prepare the tank. First, get some gravel, wash and clean it thoroughly, and put it in the bottom of the tank. Then buy some plants. There are many different varieties of suitable aquaria plants, but three good ones are *Elodea*, *Vallisneria* (Canadian pondweed;

an excellent oxygenator) and milfoil. Put the roots of your plants into the gravel and anchor them there by weighing the roots down with clean pebbles. Now put a sheet of paper carefully over the lot, pour in water slowly and gently, take out the paper (which will have prevented everything from swirling about), and then leave it all to settle. Leave it for as much as a week before you introduce the fish. The only other thing you will want is a rectangle of glass of the right size to act as a lid and keep dust out. Balancing it on something like four bits of cork at the corners will allow air to circulate freely over the surface of the water.

You must think carefully where the tank should stand. If it's to be on a polished table or any surface that could be scratched, bed it on a pad of newspaper. The windowsill may seem the obvious place to put it, but it's usually the worst, because direct sunlight will do two things: first, it will encourage the growth of algae that will make the glass or plastic sides of the tank green; and secondly, it may make the water too warm. Talking of which, don't site the tank near a fire or a radiator or heater. Round about 60 degrees Fahrenheit is a good water-temperature. And, by the way, half a dozen water-snails, which you can get from any pond, will keep down any algae.

The plants are a really important part of goldfish-keeping. Fish breathe in oxygen and breathe out carbon dioxide. Plants absorb carbon dioxide, through their leaves, and give off oxygen. Plants attract insects that the fish eat. And the fish manure the plants. So everyone's happy, and the fish have two sources of supply of the oxygen without which they cannot survive: from the air and from the plants.

Once again, the vital thing is not to overstock your tank. You can easily tell if the fish are too crowded, because they will be at the surface, gasping. If they mostly stay low in the tank, only coming to the top now and again to take food or a bubble of air, then you've got it right.

Once your fish are in the tank, provided with plants and in a suitable position, they need two things from you: to be kept clean and to be fed. Gradually a sediment will form on the bottom of the tank, made up of dead bits from the plants and fishes' droppings. This doesn't do any harm (as long as there's no stale food amongst it), but the fish can stir it up and make the water cloudy, so it's best to syphon it out occasionally, using a length of rubber tubing.

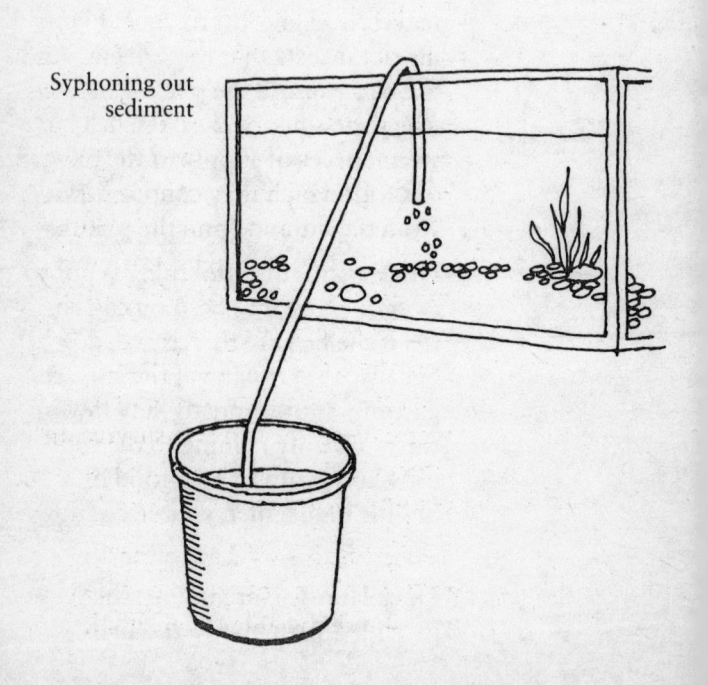

Syphoning out sediment

Goldfish 119

As for food, you can buy prepared goldfish food, and as well as this a certain amount of animal food is good for them, like small earthworms, water fleas, bloodworms and mosquito larvae. But the golden rule is don't give too much. Almost everyone tends to overfeed, and if you find you're doing so, remove any surplus or it will foul the water and affect the health of the fish. You shouldn't feed more than they can clear up in five minutes.

The other way to keep goldfish is in a garden pond. The hole for this has to be lined with concrete or polythene, or you can buy ready-made fibreglass shapes. Here, in contrast to an indoor aquarium, you'll have lots of space for more fish and for more plants to look nice and to provide more oxygen and attract more insects; and provided the water is at least a metre deep, the fish will survive, in a torpid state, under ice, unless conditions are really extreme.

The goldfish's wild ancestor is a rather dullish bronze colour, but you should be able to buy gold, yellow and silver fish, as well as fish of these colours mixed with black. And as well as Shubunkins, which are the same shape as ordinary goldfish but have more metallic scaling, there are other varieties like Twintails, Globe-eyes, and Brambleheads, which all look quite different, as their names suggest. But all these will do well in cold water, unlike the tropical varieties that are another kettle of fish altogether and need special heating. Properly looked after, your goldfish could live as long as ten years. Or more.

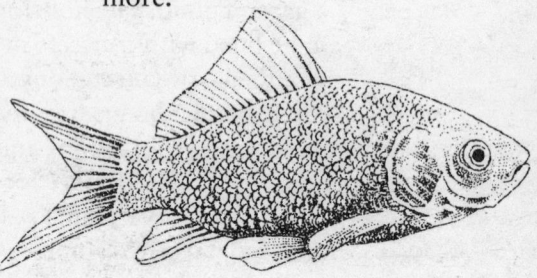

Common goldfish

I know a man who has four quite ordinary goldfish that he has never fed. They belonged first to his son but the boy grew tired of his pets and let the aquarium get dirty (just what you mustn't do). So the man, who is a breeder of prize-winning

Welsh Mountain ponies, put the four goldfish into a huge cast-iron pot, rather like a giant witch's cauldron, which stood out in the field filled with water for the ponies

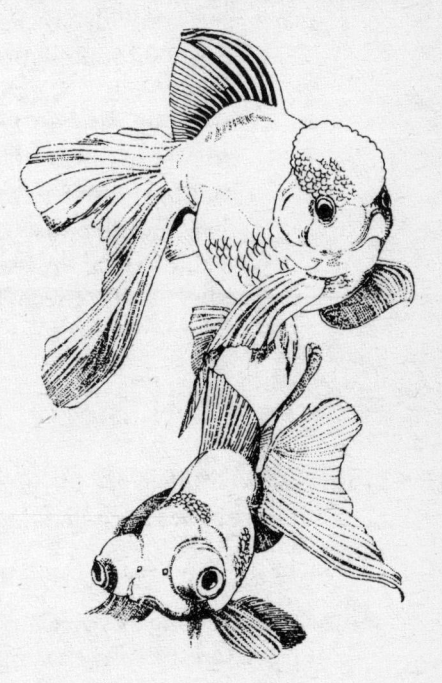

Bramblehead (*top*) and Globe-eye goldfish

to drink. It had originally been a dough-mixer, this great pot, four feet across and two and a half feet deep, and the goldfish even bred in it, had lots of babies in fact. The babies, I'm sorry to say, did not survive, for, as often happens in a garden pond, the parents ate them. And other sorts of food dropped in, in the shape of insects falling from an overhanging hedge. But almost all the food for those four fish has been provided by generations of Welsh Mountain ponies, coming to drink after eating their pony-nuts. They dip their muzzles into the great iron pot, and little bits of food that have stuck to the hair around their mouths wash off into the water to feed the fish. Pony-fed goldfish don't seem to do so badly. Those four are now fifteen years old!

Checklist

Advantages	Goldfish are silent, restful to watch, easy to keep and decorative.
Drawbacks	I can't really think of any.
Ailments	As long as you keep the water clean and the oxygen supply adequate, there's nothing to worry about.
Sexing	No way of telling him from her.
Suitable environment	Anywhere.
Lifespan	I don't know exactly. But long-lived.

12 Dogs

The dog is man's oldest animal companion and still the best-loved pet of all. More than any other pet, it comes in almost every imaginable size, shape, colour and coat. No visitor from another planet would believe that the squash-faced Pug

Pug

was any relation to the long-nosed Borzoi, that the barrel-chested, bumbling Bulldog came from the same family as the speedy, slab-sided Whippet, or that a great, shaggy St Bernard and a tiny, hairy Yorkshire Terrier could possibly belong to the same species.

It's hard to believe that the Yorkshire Terrier (*left*) and the barrel-chested Bulldog come from the same family

Man has kept the dog so long that he has been able, by selective breeding, to change it out of all recognition to its original wolf-like ancestors, and to change it in so many different ways, often for the better though sometimes very much for the worse.

But the advantage to you, if you're lucky enough to be allowed a dog of your own, lies precisely in this enormous choice. For it's not just a question of choosing a dog of the breed you fancy most. You must be certain that it will be right for the home that it's going to share with you, for ten or more years. Great Danes are not suited to life in high-rise flats, nor Chihuahuas to five-mile walks through the mud in wind and rain. What you choose must depend on where you live and why you need a dog.

Is it as a guard, like a German Shepherd or a Dobermann? Or to work, like a Border Collie or one of the gun-dogs? Or as a kind of toy, a lap dog, to be played with and fussed over, like a Pekingese or a Pomeranian? Even if your reason is none of these things, but just that you like all dogs, whether they are purebred or mongrel, and simply want one as a companion, think long and hard before you decide. And even before that, be certain in your own mind that wanting a dog isn't just a passing fancy.

Borzoi

You would be horrified if you knew how many puppies are bought, especially at Christmas time, and then discarded, often within a very short while, because their new owners have taken against them for a whole variety of reasons, sometimes simply that there have been a couple of puddles on the carpet. Then the puppy is passed on to someone else, or sold to a pet shop, or taken to the vet to be destroyed, or, perhaps worst of all, turned loose, miles from home and left to take its chances. Would you believe, for example, that anyone could throw a puppy into a river and leave it to drown?

Once my wife was walking with our German Shepherd bitch of those days, called Sadie, when she saw a van stop on a bridge in the distance. A man got out, chucked something over the parapet, and then drove hurriedly off again. Rubbish, she supposed, until she reached the bridge, and Sadie ran down the bank into the rushing water and pulled out, just in time, a choking, soaking, mongrel puppy.

That story had a happy ending, for we cared for the puppy for several weeks and then found it a good home with a kind man, but there are many stories of unwanted dogs that don't finish up so pleasantly.

But let's suppose that you're quite certain you want a dog and sure you know what kind of dog you want. The next thing to be decided is: how old should it be?

I think that the answer to this is eight weeks of age, when it is fully weaned. The dog is a highly intelligent animal and capable of learning quickly all the many things it needs to know to live in a house as a member of a family, and so it's most important that puppy and owner form a bond between each other as early as possible. Buying an older puppy means that it will have already become accustomed to someone else, the breeder perhaps, and buying a grown dog is always a gamble.

Once we were given a two-year-old Great Dane who had lived all his life in a breeding kennels. The change to becoming a house-dog was at first very puzzling and worrying for Daniel, because so many of his habits were already formed; and, indeed, throughout the long and happy life he had with us, he never barked at strangers, never ate a bone, and never learned to cock his leg but always squatted like a pup!

The training of your puppy must begin straight away, but at first it needs to be kept simple. Just as children aren't ready for proper lessons when they're very young, dogs need to be six months old or so before they can be expected to begin to master all the things they need to know. But some things must be learned right from the start, unless, for example, you want messes all over the place.

A beef marrow-bone (raw) is the best thing to stop a teething puppy from chewing up the furniture!

House-training a puppy is quite easy, provided you're prepared to work at it: this simply means putting it outside often, first thing, last thing, after each meal, and at regular intervals in between, so that it has every chance to be clean. Tell it how clever it is whenever it does anything outside, and if it should make the odd mistake inside at first, it will soon learn that you're not pleased by the scolding tone of your voice. You can even take hold of its scruff and give it a little shake as you scold — that's how its mother would discipline it — but don't ever slap it or rub its nose in it unless you want to scare and confuse it. Once cleanliness is learned, then, of course, it'll ask to go out when it needs to. The need seems to vary with the individual, and we once had a Dachshund called Anna who acted as a kind of weather forecaster. If Anna refused to go out, it meant that either it was raining or was going to rain soon; you always knew because she would disappear upstairs, sometimes for the whole of a pouring wet day. Perhaps Dachshunds have very long bladders inside their very long bodies, but you could be quite sure it was raining cats and dogs once you saw that tell-tale hump under the eiderdown.

Chewing things that shouldn't be chewed is another problem with teething puppies, and the best answer is a bone. Stick to a beef marrow-bone. Never give cooked bones, especially not of chicken or rabbit, as these can splinter and cause awful internal damage.

And the other early lessons are to teach it to know its name (a short one's much easier; for the puppy and for you) and to come when called. Later, there'll be plenty of time for all the clever stuff, sitting down and lying down and staying where it's put and walking to heel on a lead. But right from the beginning there are three things that *you* have to learn if you're to make a success of the relationship between you and your dog. They're easy to remember because they all start with the same letter.

Patience. Take it slowly – don't expect too much – don't get irritated – remember it's very young.

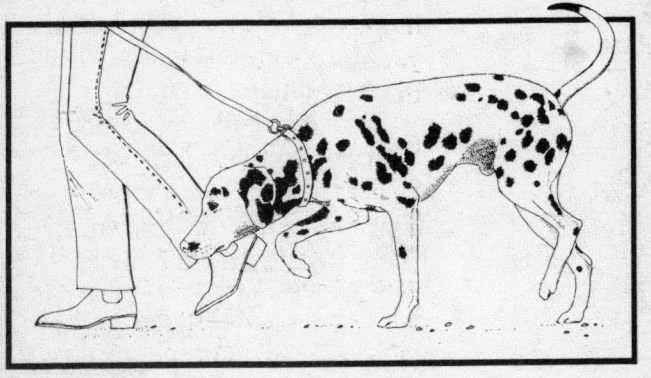

Walking a dog to heel

Perseverance. However many times it takes to teach something, the puppy must learn that it's you who's going to win: you're the boss, you're the leader of the pack.
Praise. The words 'Good dog!' are every puppy's favourites, and once it understands what you think is right, that's what it will be keen to do.

Just how much you want your dog to learn is up to you. You may be satisfied, for example, with Come and Sit and Heel; or, at the other extreme, you may decide to go to obedience classes where a dog can be taught to retrieve and to track and to find hidden objects and jump over obstacles and do all manner of clever things. But keeping a dog, any dog, is a great responsibility. It's a very different matter from owning a rabbit in a hutch, and your dog, especially if it's of a large and active breed, must be properly trained to your basic commands if it's not to become a liability to other people and a danger to itself. And remember, you have to buy a licence for your dog once it reaches the age of six months. This now costs 37½p a year.

The rules for feeding a puppy, of any breed, are roughly these: until it is three months old, give four meals a day, plus some bone-flour and a little cod liver oil (take your vet's advice on quantities of these); from three to six months, three meals a day; from six months to a year, two meals; after it is one year old, one meal a day is enough. And the size of the meal depends on the size of the dog.

Once we had a lot of spare duck eggs that we fed to another of our Great Danes, called Humphrey, for his supper. Looking back, it was a stupid thing to do (though luckily he came to no harm) because there were thirty eggs in that omelette.

But remember that this pet is a carnivore and so should be fed mainly on meat. Some milk and the occasional egg are good, especially in the growing stages, and a certain amount of biscuit, but meat is what is best for dogs' health. Plenty of meat and plenty of exercise – that's what they need, just as their wolfish ancestors did.

Consult your vet about inoculations (which simply *must* be

done, in fairness to your dog and everyone else's) and about worming. Some vets prefer to give the first inoculation at ten weeks, some at twelve. A well-reared puppy will have been wormed a couple of times by the breeder before it is eight weeks old, and you'll probably be advised to worm a third time at three months.

On one thing I'm certainly not going to try to advise you, and that is what breed of dog to select. The value of any dog lies in the character of the individual, not in the breeding or lack of breeding. The most unforgettable dog I ever had was a very small, grumpy, hairy, black-and-white, short-legged terrier called Susie; she cost me two packets of Woodbine cigarettes. In her lifetime, she was badly bitten by a bulldog, poisoned, buried alive in a badger sett for eight bitter winter days and nights, run over by a van, run over by a car, and almost died having, at an advanced age, her one and only puppy. At last, just before her fourteenth birthday, Susie was hit by an express train as she chased a fox across the railway lines, and that was too much, even for her.

Your dog, I hope, will have a less dramatic life, but it can only have a really happy one if it is properly treated, treated, that is to say, as probably the most intelligent, affectionate, and trusting sort of pet that you could ever be lucky enough to own. I'm lucky enough to own five at the moment, a German Shepherd, a small Terrier (like Susie, but smooth-coated), and three miniature wire-haired Dachshunds, one of which you can see on the front cover of this book. Her name, as you may know, is Dodo.

Checklist

Advantages Of all usual pets, the dog must be the most rewarding to keep. Handsome or quaint or just plain ugly, it is intelligent, trainable, and loyal. It has many uses and in some cases is indispensable (guide-dog for the blind). More than any other pet, it becomes a family member and even the smallest dog is the best possible deterrent against intruders.

Drawbacks	Some breeds, especially the smaller ones, can be very yappy, and any dog that is not under control can be a nuisance, sometimes a grave one. If you live in sheep-farming country, you must be careful to keep your dog under control. Sheep-worrying is a serious problem for farmers, and they can legally shoot a dog if they can prove that it has been worrying their sheep.
Ailments	Dogs are susceptible to virus diseases like distemper, hard pad and Parvo, so must have their inoculations and boosters in due course. Some simple conditions, diarrhoea for example, can be dealt with by you (starve for a day, then give digestive biscuits and Ambrosia creamed rice for a couple of days), but the best rule for things like eczema, mange or anything you're worried about is: when in doubt, consult your vet.
Sexing	Unlike kittens, it's quite easy to tell male and female puppies apart (see diagram on p. 137).
Suitable environment	You must use your common sense. Big dogs generally need big houses

	with big gardens. Any breed will live happily in the country, but not all are suitable for town life.
Lifespan	As a very general rule, the bigger the dog the shorter the life expectation. Ten is a good age for a Great Dane, but one of the granddaughters of my little terrier Susie lived to nineteen, and much older dogs have been recorded.
Useful periodicals	*Our Dogs* (weekly). *Dog World* (weekly).

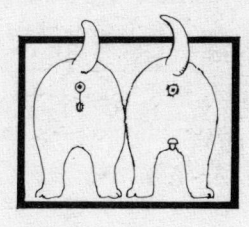

Female   Male

Further reading

ALLCOCK, JAMES. *A Pet Bird of Your Own*, Sheldon Press, 1981

DENHAM, KEN. *Guinea-pigs and Chinchillas*, J. Bartholomew, 1977

FINN, F. W. *Pets and How to Keep Them*, Hutchinson & Co., 1907

GORDON, JOHN. *Dogs*, J. Bartholomew, 1976

HUTCHINSON, PATRICIA. *Beginner's Guide to Guinea-pigs*, Paradise Press, 1983

KAY, DAVID. *Bantams*, David & Charles, 1983

NIGHTINGALE, GAY. *Rabbit Keeping*, J. Bartholomew, 1982

POND, GRACE *and* SAYERS, ANGELA. *Cats*, J. Bartholomew, 1982

POPE, JOYCE. *The Young Pet Owner's Handbook*, Purnell & Sons, 1981

ROBINSON, DAVID. *Hamsters and Gerbils*, Spur Publications, 1979

ROGERS, CYRIL. *Budgerigars*, J. Bartholomew, 1976

R.S.P.C.A.* *Pet Guide: Care for Your Cat*, Collins, 1980

SMITH, K. W. *Mice and Rats*, J. Bartholomew, 1976

SNOW, C. F. *Rabbit Keeping*, W. & G. Foyle, 1961

---

* As well as *Care for Your Cat*, the RSPCA produces booklets on most of the other pets mentioned in this book, and a quarterly magazine, *Animal World*. You can get more information about the RSPCA publications and the RSPCA Junior Membership by sending a stamped-addressed envelope to RSPCA Junior Membership, Causeway, Horsham, Sussex RH12 1HG.